your OCD will hate this book

your OCD will *hate* this book

A Proven System to Overcome Obsessive-Compulsive Disorder and Take Back Your Life

Nathan Peterson

Vermilion
LONDON

VERMILION

UK | USA | Canada | Ireland | Australia
India | New Zealand | South Africa

Vermilion is part of the Penguin Random House group of companies
whose addresses can be found at global.penguinrandomhouse.com

Penguin Random House UK
One Embassy Gardens, 8 Viaduct Gardens, London SW11 7BW

penguin.co.uk

Penguin Random House UK

First published in the United States by Plume,
an imprint of Penguin Random House LLC in 2026
First published in Great Britain by Vermilion in 2026
1

Typeset by Six Red Marbles UK, Thetford, Norfolk

Printed and bound in Great Britain by Clays Ltd, Elcograf S.p.A.

The information in this book has been compiled as general guidance on the specific subjects addressed. It is not a substitute and not to be relied on for medical, healthcare or pharmaceutical professional advice. Please consult your GP before changing, stopping or starting any medical treatment. So far as the author is aware the information given is correct and up to date as at April 2026. Practice, laws and regulations all change and the reader should obtain up to date professional advice on any such issues. The author and publishers disclaim, as far as the law allows, any liability arising directly or indirectly from the use or misuse of the information contained in this book.

The authorised representative in the EEA is Penguin Random House Ireland,
Morrison Chambers, 32 Nassau Street, Dublin D02 YH68

A CIP catalogue record for this book is available from the British Library

ISBN 9781785046728

Penguin Random House is committed to a sustainable future
for our business, our readers and our planet. This book is made
from Forest Stewardship Council® certified paper.

FSC www.fsc.org MIX Paper FSC® C018179

For Gina, who never doubted

For my mom, who showed me how to be kind

And for my brother, my guide into
the OCD community

contents

your OCD will hate this book

Introduction

What Is OCD, Really?

Let's get straight to it. You picked up this book because OCD is messing with your life, and you want to know what to do about it. Not just understand it, but actually do something about it.

As a licensed clinical social worker who specializes in this condition, I've worked one-on-one with hundreds of people with OCD, and I have guided hundreds of thousands more through my YouTube channel. Let me tell you something straight up: There is treatment that works. Not fancy theories, not endless talking about your feelings, but real guidance that can help you get your life back.

Here's the Thing About OCD

Let me introduce you to Sarah. She's sitting in my office right now, and man, she's tired. Tired of the thoughts that won't go away. Tired of doing things she knows logically don't make sense. Honestly, she's tired of having hope that she can find some relief only to be swindled once again.

"But I don't know if I even have OCD," she tells me.

Sound familiar? There are a lot of misconceptions about OCD. It isn't just about being super clean or about keeping your things nice and tidy. It's about getting stuck. And I mean *stuck*.

You get these thoughts, maybe about harm, maybe about contamination, maybe about your relationship, about who you are as a person and if you'd really do that thing it tells you that you are capable of doing. Your brain keeps screaming that you need to do something about these thoughts right now. So you do whatever you can to make the thoughts go away. You check things. You ask for reassurance. You avoid stuff. You analyze everything and ruminate about every possibility.

So let's make this super simple. You might have OCD if:

1. Your brain keeps throwing unwanted thoughts, images, or urges at you that:
    - Won't leave you alone
    - Make you question and second-guess yourself
    - Go against everything you actually want or believe

2. You feel like you *have* to do certain things to:
    - Make the thoughts stop
    - Prevent something bad from happening
    - Gain certainty that what you're experiencing is false

3. And all this:
    - Takes up way too much of your day
    - Gets in the way of living your life the way you want
    - Feels impossible to control, even though you know it's OCD

Here's a wild thing about OCD: It goes after what matters most to you. You're a loving parent? Boom, ruminations about harming your kid. Super religious? Here come the blasphemous thoughts. In a great relationship? Get ready for endless doubts about your partner. Think about yourself and the things you truly care about. I would bet this is what OCD is latching on to.

Why This Book Is Different

If you're looking for a book that just explains OCD and the science behind it, this might not be the one for you. This book is about doing something about it. That's what treatment is all about.

This book is like having me, an OCD therapist, right there with you. I'm going to show you exactly what to do, step by step. No complex terms, no long explanations, just straight talk and real tools you can use right now.

I am going to show you how Sarah and I tackled this together and how she maintains the progress that she's made and lives exactly how she wants to.

If you don't think we'll address your OCD theme or fear, don't worry. I've got you covered. What's neat about Sarah is that her theme changes, allowing us to explore how someone would do treatment for each common OCD fear. But as you'll soon learn, your fear may not matter as much as you think.

This book can help you whether you:

- Are already working with a therapist
- Are stuck on a waiting list
- Can't get to therapy right now
- Have worked with a therapist before and are trying to maintain your progress

You're in the right place and I've got you. We're going to do this together.

Real Talk About Treatment

Here's something you need to know right now: Talking about OCD won't fix it. Understanding OCD won't fix it. Even reading this book won't fix it, unless you do the work.

It's like going to the gym. Reading about workouts won't give you muscles. You've got to lift the weights. Treatment is the same way. I'm going to show you exactly what to do, but you've got to show up and do it.

"But I'm not ready."

"But what if . . . ?"

"But my OCD is different."

Nah, we're not doing that. OCD loves those buts and it loves to wait. It loves making excuses. You know why? Because if it can stop you from doing treatment, it can continue to live. I know that's not what you want. I'll teach you how to integrate this treatment into all aspects of your life and help you find the motivation to do some tough things.

How This Book Works

All of that means this isn't just a book you read. It's a treatment protocol you'll actually *do*. Every chapter builds on the previous one, walking you through the exact same process I use with people like Sarah in my office.

You're getting worksheets. Real ones. The same ones I use with my clients. We've got:

- OCD symptom tracker to figure out exactly what we're dealing with
- Understanding OCD's playbook to keep you one step ahead
- Identifying your core fear and connecting to your values
- Motivational exercises to keep you going
- Self-compassion strategies for the rough moments
- Mindfulness tools to stay grounded
- Hierarchy worksheet to plan your exposures
- Goal-setting tools to keep you on track
- Script-writing worksheet for your toughest fears

- Treatment planners to make this actually happen
- Aftercare guides for when you're rocking it

I'm going to walk you through every single step. We'll start with the basics and build up to the tough stuff. You'll see how Sarah does it, and you'll do it right alongside her.

No more wondering what to do next. No more guessing if you're doing it right. I'm going to show you exactly how to use every tool, every worksheet, every strategy.

Ready? Let's go. I know without a doubt that you can do this.

Chapter 1

Your Brain's False Alarm System

"I'm up by four thirty, and I don't leave for work until eight," Sarah confesses, hands wrapped tight in her sleeves. Her voice quivers slightly. "Three hours . . . just washing my hands."

I nod, taking this in. Three hours of handwashing. Every morning.

Wait, wait, wait. Sigh . . .

I need to pause our story for a second.

I know what you're thinking as you read this. "Really? Another OCD expert using handwashing as an example? How original."

Look, it pains me to use contamination. Trust me. I almost rolled my eyes writing this. But here's the deal—it's the one we all understand. Everyone's seen someone wash their hands or avoid touching something "dirty." It's simple to follow. And this book? This book is all about keeping things simple.

So yes, I'm going to tell you about Sarah and her contamination OCD. But as you read, I need you to do something important.

I need *you* to think about your own OCD theme. Maybe you're dealing with harm thoughts that won't go away. Maybe you're stuck analyzing your relationship for the millionth time. Maybe you're questioning your faith, your identity, whether you're a good person, or if you turned off the stove (even though you checked multiple times). Whatever your theme is, the same cycle is running the show. The specific fear may be different, but the game is exactly the same.

Now, back to Sarah in my office, who's watching me expectantly, waiting for a solution to her three-hour morning ritual.

"We will get to a solution," I assure her. "But first, I need to understand exactly what's happening."

Why Your Brain Won't Be Quiet

"Okay," Sarah says, fidgeting with her sleeve again. She looks down at her hands, red and raw from over-washing. "But how does this thing even work? Because it feels like my brain is just . . . broken."

I lean forward in my chair. This question is crucial.

"Not broken," I tell her firmly. "Just stuck. Think of it like a smoke detector that's become too sensitive."

Sarah's eyebrows rise slightly.

"You know how a properly functioning smoke detector only goes off when there's actual fire or dangerous smoke?"

I continue. "But yours has become so sensitive that it screams every time you cook, light a candle, or even take a hot shower."

A small smile forms at the corners of Sarah's mouth as if she knows exactly what I'm talking about.

"That's what's happening in your brain right now," I explain. "It's sounding the alarm for everything, treating normal thoughts like they're emergencies when they're really just . . . burnt toast."

Sarah nods slowly, considering this. "So my brain is like . . . a smoke detector that thinks every little bit of steam is smoke?"

I laugh. "Exactly! It's doing its job, trying to protect you, but it's lost the ability to tell the difference between real danger and everyday life."

Let's break down exactly what happened to Sarah this morning, and I want you to think about how this same cycle shows up in your life.

The Trigger (the Thing That Starts It All)

Sarah takes a deep breath and describes the moment that everything started to go wrong: "I touched my doorknob to leave for work."

"And then what popped into your head?" I prompt. "How did your brain say you were in danger?"

Her eyes dart to the side, slightly embarrassed. "The thought that it might be covered in germs that could make me sick." She looks up suddenly. "But everyone thinks about germs sometimes, right? Why does my brain get so stuck on it?"

Sarah's doorknob is the trigger that starts it all. She's right: Everyone does have random thoughts about germs, harm, mortality, or who they are as a person. But not everyone spends three hours each morning washing their hands. It's OCD that blows these thoughts out of proportion and makes them stick.

These triggers come in different forms:

Intrusive thoughts: These are those thoughts that we don't want, but they keep coming back anyway.

- "What if I get sick?"
- "What if I hurt someone?"
- "What if I'm not really in love?"
- "What if I sinned?"
- "What if I'm a bad person?"
- "What if I'm losing my mind?"
- "What if I'm living the wrong life?"
- "What if I'm a terrible person?"
- "What if I can't stop noticing my breathing?"
- "What if I lose control?"
- "What if nothing is real?"
- "What if I made the wrong choice?"

"Do any of these sound familiar?" I ask Sarah.

"Yeah," she admits quietly. "A lot of them, actually. My triggers aren't just thoughts, though."

Sarah is right—triggers come in many forms.

I want to see if you, reader, can relate to these common triggers.

Memories: A time you got sick years ago, that moment you lost your temper, a conversation in which you might have offended someone, something inappropriate you did as a kid, a mistake you made at work, or a time you weren't entirely honest.

Urges or impulses: A sudden feeling like you might yell in church, push someone off a platform, or harm yourself.

Images: Mental pictures that pop into your head, like seeing yourself doing something violent, picturing a loved one getting hurt, seeing sexual images, visualizing a tragic accident, seeing yourself acting inappropriately in public, or imagining contamination spreading across your body.

Ideas: Random thoughts, like thinking your memories might be fake, feeling that you're secretly evil deep down, wondering if you're living in a dream, believing you caused something bad to happen, doubting your own existence, or questioning if you've been good your whole life.

Sensations: Physical feelings like your heart racing, your breathing patterns, your hands feeling sticky, arousal, or something just not feeling right.

I glance back at Sarah. She's sitting straighter now, eyes wide with recognition.

"I didn't realize all of those things could be triggers," she says.

"Most people don't," I tell her. "That's why OCD can be so sneaky."

Listen up, reader. Think about your own triggers right now. Maybe you're sitting there thinking, "Well, Nate . . . you didn't mention mine exactly how I experience it, so my OCD must be different." Trust me, it's not. We'll go over later why OCD uses this big fat lie to keep you stuck.

The Faulty Threat Detector

I can see the gears turning in Sarah's head as she shifts in her chair, leaning forward. "But why does my brain treat a doorknob like it's a live grenade?" Her hands twist together in her lap.

This is where it gets interesting. I smile and lean back slightly.

"Let me tell you about my little dog, Gunner," I start, and Sarah relaxes a bit at the change of subject. "He's a shorkie. Part Yorkie and part shih tzu."

"Cute," Sarah offers.

"Adorable," I agree. "And he barks at the slightest thing. He's constantly on alert, staring at the door, waiting for danger. And here's the thing—he's nine years old and hasn't once, not a single time, gotten the threat right."

Sarah laughs.

"But it doesn't matter," I continue. "No matter how many times we tell him to stop barking, he's going to do what he thinks is best. Even if he's wrong."

I tap the desk gently for emphasis. "This is exactly like the faulty threat detector in your brain. It's trying to figure out what's a real threat and what isn't. So just in case, it sends off the alarms—better safe than sorry, right? Even though it's never actually caught a real threat, it keeps on barking."

"But my brain . . ." Sarah starts, then stops, searching for words.

"Is just like Gunner," I finish for her. "Treating many thoughts like they are emergencies. *Danger! Emergency! Everyone panic!* Even though it's been wrong every single time."

Let's go through the OCD cycle together. This is an important visual to help you understand how your brain learns to keep you stuck in problem-solving mode.

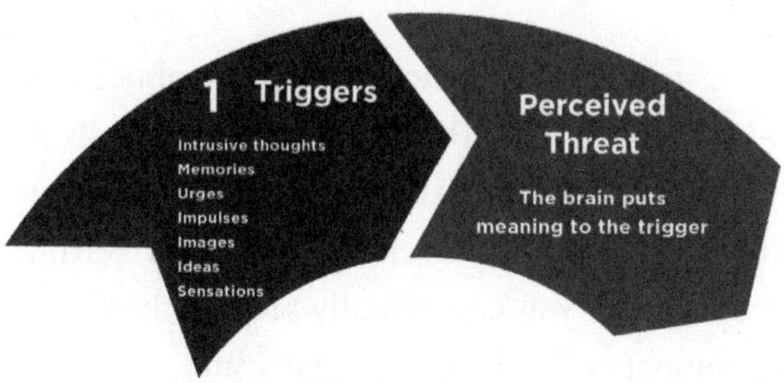

This is what we call the perceived threat, when Sarah's brain—or yours—puts meaning on a trigger. It's like having a really bad translator that turns everything into worst-case scenarios.

Everyone's brain does this sort of assessment every day, filtering out what's important and what's not. Imagine your email's spam filter broke. Usually, only the important stuff gets through, while junk gets filtered out automatically. But now everything floods your inbox—real emails, scams, random ads—and you're stuck frantically sorting through every single message, treating each one like it could be urgent.

In your brain, thoughts that would normally be thrown into the "not important" pile get shuffled into the "I'm not sure, so let me send the alarms, just in case" pile.

Look, your brain has a lot of information to sift through. That's why it's your job to retrain it to stop seeing unnecessary threats and put that darn filter back where it belongs.

Brain without OCD: "That's just a doorknob."
Brain with OCD: "*Danger! Alert!* Just in case . . . go wash your hands."

Take a moment right now and think about how your OCD brain interprets a threat. Can you physically see it? Is it obvious? Or is it just a feeling? A guess? Or you're not sure?

This is where OCD takes flight. It's not warning you about the things you can actually see. It's there for you in those moments when you're not quite sure.

If you just thought to yourself, "But I don't know if I could tell the difference between a real threat and an OCD threat," you're not alone. This is exactly what OCD wants you to question.

Here Comes the Anxiety

Let's get to the next part of that cycle:

Once your brain labels something as a threat, your body does exactly what it's supposed to do: It responds to the danger. Sarah knows that feeling.

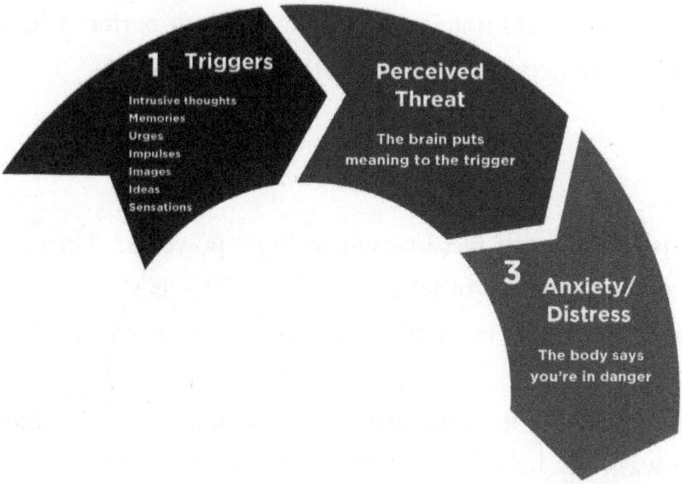

"It's like my whole body goes into panic mode," she explains, gesturing to demonstrate. "My heart races, I start to feel hot and I can't think straight . . ."

Sarah's body is doing its job well. If there actually *was* a deadly virus on that doorknob, this response would be super helpful. The problem is that without real evidence, it is responding to a false alarm, just like my dog barking at its own shadow.

Sarah gives a half smile at this image.

"So . . . my body's doing what it's supposed to . . . just at the wrong time?"

"Precisely," I say, impressed with her insight. "And that's crucial to understand because it's what drives everything that follows."

Think about your own anxiety response. Notice how your body reacts when OCD triggers show up. That racing heart? The tightness in your chest? The desperate need to *do something*? That's not a malfunction. It's your perfectly functioning anxiety system responding to a false alarm.

The Urge to Fix It

False alarms can feel overwhelmingly powerful. They can overshadow every other thing in life. This is that fight-or-flight that kicks in. It screams, "Do something now! Why risk it?"

This moment, in Sarah's words, is when "I feel like I *have* to wash my hands." Her voice takes on an urgent quality. She demonstrates with a quick rubbing motion, her hands

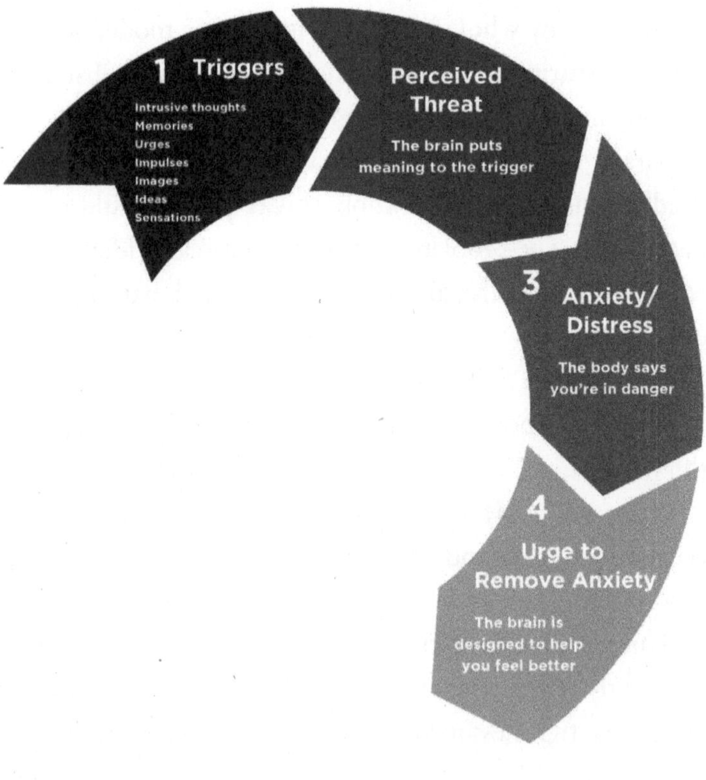

moving almost automatically. "Like, if I don't, something terrible will happen."

I hold up my own hand gently, interrupting her phantom washing. I wait a moment for her to focus, then I continue. "Sarah, imagine you're hiking and suddenly see a bear on the trail."

Her eyes widen. "I'd run!"

"Exactly! Your anxiety kicks in and your brain immediately serves up solutions: Back away slowly! Make yourself big! Get out of here!"

"But there's no bear on my doorknob," she says, getting it.

"No, but your brain can't tell the difference," I explain. "The anxiety signal feels identical whether you're facing a bear or touching a doorknob. So, it starts throwing solutions at you: 'Wash your hands! No, wash them again! Check the soap expiration date! Google deadly doorknob germs! Ask someone if you're going to be okay!' "

This is Sarah's emergency response system kicking in. When you're anxious, your brain is designed to:

1. Identify the threat (Contaminated doorknob!)

2. Create a plan (Must wash hands!)

3. Make you follow through (*Now!*)

4. Make you repeat it (Just in case, maybe go do it again.)

Your brain is rarely satisfied and urges you to keep going

until you know you're safe. But as my friend Admiral Ackbar says, "It's a trap!"

The Things We Do to Feel Safe (Compulsions)

"This is where it gets tricky," I explain, pointing at the next section of the cycle. "Your brain is screaming for you to do something, anything, to make the anxiety go away. So, you do compulsions."

I look directly at Sarah. "But what OCD actually wants is certainty."

Take a moment and think about your specific fear. Consider all the compulsions you do. What are you really trying to achieve? Aren't you just trying to know for sure?

Sarah nods slowly, her eyes fixed on a point in the distance as she processes this. "I just want to know I won't get sick," she says quietly. "That I won't make anyone else sick."

"Exactly," I tell her, leaning forward. "Your brain is designed to want certainty—it's how we survive. But OCD takes this normal need to know things and cranks it up to impossible levels. Even when you logically know something, OCD finds a way to doubt it."

I gesture toward her, inviting more. "Walk me through what you did after touching the doorknob this morning."

Sarah takes a deep breath. "Well . . . first I washed my hands. But then I worried I didn't use enough soap, so I washed them again. Then I used hand sanitizer." Her words start coming faster. "Then I worried the sanitizer might be expired, so I washed again. Then I had to change my clothes because what if germs got on them while I was washing? Then I had to clean the sink because I touched it while my hands were dirty. . . ."

I nod. "See what's happening? Each compulsion is an attempt to gain absolute certainty. But here's the problem: You can never be a hundred percent certain about anything. There's always room for doubt if you look hard enough. And OCD is really, really good at finding doubt."

Compulsions look different for each person. The common thread is that they're all ways for you to feel a sense of certainty, or attempt to completely eradicate a feeling of anxiety, guilt, or shame.

As you read through these common compulsions, I want you to keep track of any you might do. Write them down. Keep this list handy, as we'll be using it later.

PHYSICAL ACTIONS

- Washing and cleaning
- Checking things repeatedly
- Checking your body for symptoms or changes
- Arranging or organizing
- Tapping or touching
- Counting or repeating actions

MENTAL RITUALS

- Reviewing memories
- Analyzing thoughts
- Counting in your head
- Silent praying
- "Canceling out" bad thoughts

BEHAVIORAL CHANGES

- Steering clear of triggers
- Not touching certain things

- Avoiding certain places
- Procrastinating decisions

SEEKING REASSURANCE

- Asking others if you're okay
- Googling your thoughts
- Confessing thoughts or actions
- Checking and rechecking

Back in my office, Sarah points to several items on my list. She acknowledges that she does a lot of these things, not just the washing. Most people with OCD do.

We Taught OCD It Was Right

I look at Sarah, who's been quiet for a moment. "And did the washing work?" I ask.

She lets out a bitter laugh, shaking her head. "Yeah, for like . . . five minutes. Then I started thinking about all the surfaces I touched while washing my hands, and it started all over again."

This is the cruel joke of OCD. The compulsions work! They really do . . . for about a minute. Or sometimes only a microsecond. You get that sweet hit of relief. Your brain says, "Phew, you're now safe. Good job!"

But it's temporary. Super temporary. Because the problem isn't the doorknob, the thought, or whatever triggered you. The problem is that your brain's guard dog won't stop barking.

This is where OCD really shows its genius. Every time you do a compulsion and get that brief relief, you're teaching your brain two things:

1. It was correct that the doorknob was dangerous. Why else would you have needed to wash your hands six times?

2. You were smart to listen to it, and you should remember for next time: Washing equals safety.

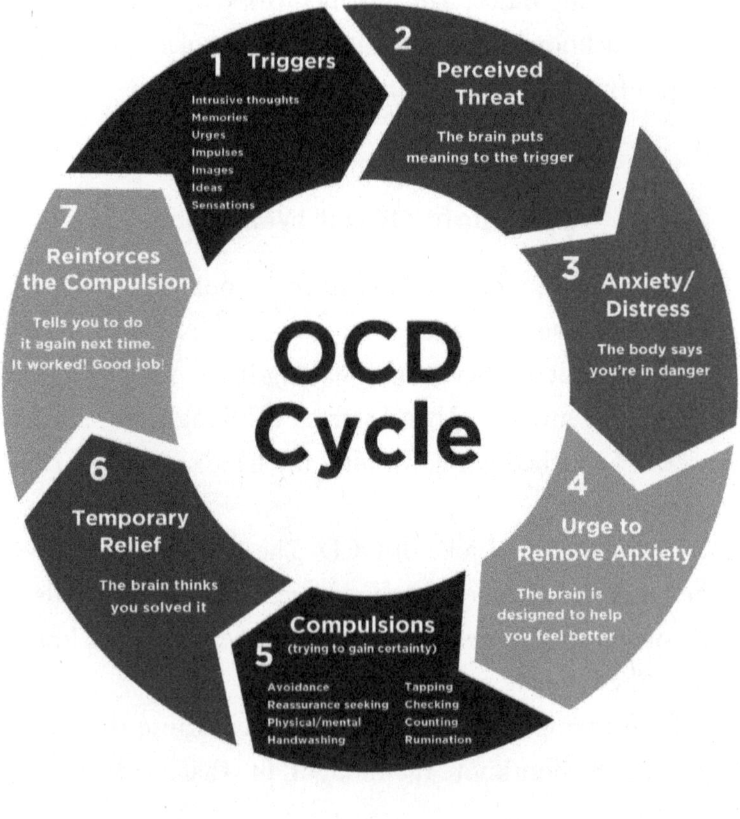

Here are the final two stages of our cycle. Or, as I explain them to Sarah, "Your brain thinks it's learning an important survival lesson. But really, it's just getting better at being afraid."

Sarah starts to understand. "So, when I wash my hands . . . my brain's guard dog gets a treat?"

"Yep! It says, 'Good job barking! Keep it up! Clearly that was super dangerous!' "

Her face falls. "And that's why I spent three hours washing this morning," she says quietly.

We've Got to Teach Your Brain Something New

Sarah looks up at me, exhausted. Her shoulders slump forward. "I can't keep doing this," she says quietly. "Three hours of my life, gone. Just like that." She pauses, frustration crossing her face. "I mean, I know it's ridiculous. I know there isn't a threat, but I do it anyway."

I lean forward, making sure she hears this next part clearly.

"You're right," I tell her. "You can't keep doing this. And you don't have to. But we're not going to fix this by figuring out why you have OCD or by analyzing every thought. We're going to fix it by retraining that overprotective guard dog of yours."

Now I want to speak directly to you, the reader.

I want you—yes, *you*, reading this right now—to grab a pen and paper. This isn't just busywork. This is the beginning of your treatment.

Write down your answers to these questions:

- What sets off my brain's alarm system? (triggers)
- What meaning does my guard dog put on it? (meaning)
- What do I do to try to feel safe? (compulsions)
- How long does the relief last?
- How has this cycle taken over my life?

Wait . . . are you still reading? If so, I assume you already answered these questions in detail. Right?

Because once you see the setup, you can start breaking free. And here's the thing: OCD isn't just some random collection of thoughts and urges. It's smart. It's sneaky. It has specific ways to keep you stuck in this cycle. Once we learn these, we're going to use them later to fight back.

"So this can actually change?" Sarah asks, a glimmer of hope in her eyes. "My brain can learn something different?"

"Absolutely," I assure her. (And you don't get many assurances with OCD!)

And yours can too, reader.

Look, I know understanding how your OCD works isn't the fun part. The action part, the actual treatment where you start taking your life back—that's coming soon. That's the good stuff. But we've got to get through this understanding piece first. It's like learning the rules of a game before you can play it (and eventually win it).

In the next chapter, we're going to pull back the curtain on how OCD really works.

You'll learn its favorite tricks, how it uses uncertainty against you, and why running away from the anxiety only makes it stronger. But don't worry, we're not going to stay here long. Just enough to know what we're dealing with. Then we'll get to the part where you actually do something about it.

Chapter 2

What Makes OCD Tick?

Here's one of the biggest eye-openers for my clients: OCD is a liar. Not just occasionally wrong, but actively and persistently deceptive. It's like a full-time con artist living in your head.

"OCD . . . lies?" Sarah looks skeptical during our second session.

"Constantly," I tell her. "It's actually OCD's favorite hobby. And it's really, really good at it."

Think about that friend who's completely charming but utterly unreliable. They make promises they never keep, but they're so convincing, you believe them every time.

"Oh, I have a cousin like that." Sarah nods. "He once convinced me to lend him money because he was 'definitely' getting a huge tax refund the next day. I'm still waiting for that refund three years later."

That's Sarah's OCD. Except instead of borrowing money,

it's stealing her time, energy, and peace of mind. The million-dollar question, of course, is: Why is OCD so darn convincing? If it's just a false alarm, why does it feel so real? And why do we keep falling for it, time and time again?

That's what we're tackling in this chapter. We're breaking down how OCD operates, to see exactly what makes it tick. And once you understand what's happening, you'll be in a much better position to start fighting back.

Lies, Lies, and More Lies: OCD's Playbook

OCD tells specific lies that are so predictable, I can practically recite them before my clients do. Let me share with you some of the most common ones:

"If you feel anxious about something, it must be dangerous."

Oh, your heart's racing after touching that doorknob? Clearly *it must be covered in deadly supergerms. Couldn't possibly be your anxiety response. Nope. Definitely imminent death.*

"If you think something is terrible, it means you secretly want it to happen."

Because obviously that random thought about your car veering off the road means you're secretly planning to crash. Just like how thinking about pizza means you'll definitely order one. Every. Single. Time.

"Better safe than sorry . . . always."

This one sounds so reasonable! Like checking your tire pressure before a road trip. Except OCD's version of "better safe than sorry" means checking the stove seventy-four times, then taking a video of it being off, then calling a neighbor to verify, then turning your car around when you're halfway to work just to check again. You know, totally normal safety precautions!

"You can achieve 100 percent certainty if you just try hard enough."

Like promising "just one more check" will finally make you sure. It's OCD's version of "just five more minutes" on your alarm clock, except it's been going off for three hours and you're still hitting snooze.

"This fear is different from your other fears."

Sure, OCD's track record is 0 for 863, but this *thought is totally legit.*

"Last time was your OCD; this time it's real."

The ultimate gaslighting. "Those six hundred other times were your OCD, but this *worry is totally legitimate. You're just being cautious!" It's like a burglar trying to convince you that the alarm going off is just a system test. OCD loves to use this one because if it can convince you that this time the danger is real, you'll keep checking, keep avoiding, keep doing compulsions—and it gets to stick around.*

How many of these sound familiar? Probably most of them. That's because, regardless of your theme, OCD uses the same playbook. Whether you're dealing with contamination fears, relationship doubts, or harm thoughts, OCD's tactics are remarkably consistent.

Whenever I release a video on YouTube I see people in the comments who are shocked because I was able to explain their OCD exactly how they experience it. "It's like he's in my head," they say. But I'll let you in on a little secret. Because OCD doesn't deviate from its typical tricks, I can guess pretty accurately how someone is experiencing it. The cool part is that this predictable playbook will be to our advantage once we get to treatment.

I want you to start noticing these lies when they pop up. Call them out. "That's just OCD lying again." The more you can spot the deception, the less power it has over you.

Uncertainty: OCD's Favorite Fuel

"Here's what OCD is really about," I tell Sarah. "Certainty. OCD makes you feel like you need to be a hundred percent sure about things when that's just not possible."

Remember the OCD cycle? Let's see exactly how uncertainty fuels it to keep it all going.

1. You touch a doorknob.

2. Your brain zeroes in on the *uncertainty*:
   "Could there be dangerous germs on it?
   I don't know for sure!"

3. This uncertainty immediately creates *anxiety*—your brain hates not knowing.

4. To escape this uncomfortable uncertainty, you do *compulsions* (like washing).

5. Washing gives you *temporary relief* from uncertainty. ("Okay, now I'm safe.")

6. This teaches your brain that uncertainty is dangerous and compulsions fix it, *reinforcing* the whole cycle.

The entire cycle revolves around escaping uncertainty. Every compulsion you do is really an attempt to become certain about something your brain has transformed from "I don't know for sure" into "*Danger: Must resolve now!*"

And yet, everyone faces uncertainty every day. We all encounter situations where we can't be 100 percent sure about things. The difference isn't you . . . it's OCD.

OCD takes normal uncertainty and transforms it into an emergency. It doesn't matter if it's about germs, relationships, morality, or anything else; the specific content is just a mask OCD wears.

So far, I've used contamination examples in this book, but I could swap them for any other OCD theme and the pattern would be identical. The pattern is what matters: OCD flags something normal as dangerous, then promises that compulsions will give you all the answers. It is, of course, a false promise, like chasing the horizon.

I've seen these same patterns play out with lots of different themes. I've had many patients with harm OCD, in which, despite being gentle, caring people, they have horrifying intrusive thoughts about hurting their loved ones. Their OCD would use the same playbook: It would insist their anxiety means danger, that these thoughts reveal something about their true character, and that they need to mentally review every interaction to be "sure" they haven't caused harm.

Different theme, same OCD pattern of turning "maybe" into "danger."

That's why we don't treat different OCD themes differently. We don't need separate treatment plans for contamination OCD, relationship OCD, and harm OCD. We treat OCD as OCD, because underneath all the different masks, it's the same disorder playing the same tricks.

This is actually good news! It means you're not broken, and your specific fears aren't the problem. OCD works the same way for everyone. And that means the solution works for everyone too.

Throw Logic out the Window

Ever try to reason with your OCD? How'd that work out for you?

Not great, right?

That's because OCD has a counterargument for everything. It's like debating a lawyer who's had years to prepare their case against your five minutes of desperate thinking.

"I try to talk myself out of washing my hands," Sarah admits. "I tell myself it's excessive. But then my brain just says, 'Yeah, but what if this time there really *are* dangerous germs? Better safe than sorry!' "

"Exactly!" I say. "It's like playing a board game with a six-year-old who changes the rules at the very last minute when they know they're losing."

I've heard these excuses so many times from clients that I can practically predict what OCD will say next. Here are some of its favorite comebacks:

"Just do it now and you can focus on other things."

This efficiency argument sounds so reasonable! Just wash your hands for ten minutes and then you can enjoy your day. Except it's never just ten minutes, is it?

"Any normal person would check again."

Ah, peer pressure from imaginary reasonable people. (Spoiler alert: They wouldn't.)

"You deserve the compulsion, you've had a hard day."

The self-care trap. OCD disguises itself as your compassionate friend, as if compulsions are treats rather than traps.

"You want to sleep tonight, right?"

This threat leverages your other needs against you. Sure, don't do the compulsion . . . if you want to lie awake all night thinking about it!

"You're not ready for treatment anyway."

This discouragement keeps you from even attempting treatment. Whether you're stressed about finals, your kids, or your job, this argument says now just isn't a good time to fight OCD. Maybe next month when things calm down. (Spoiler: Things rarely "calm down" enough for OCD to give you permission to start treatment.)

Think about the last time you felt compelled to do a compulsion. What justification did your OCD use to convince you? Was it on this list?

Avoiding Fear Makes OCD Happy

"There's another piece to this puzzle," I tell Sarah. "OCD thrives on avoidance."

Fear drives avoidance. And avoidance strengthens fear. It's a vicious cycle that keeps OCD alive and well.

"After I touched that doorknob," Sarah admits, "I started using my sleeve to open doors. I thought I was being clever, finding a work-around."

"But what message did that send to your brain?" I ask.

She thinks for a moment. "That doorknobs are dangerous and need to be avoided."

Sarah is exactly right. Each time she avoids something because of her OCD fears, she's basically giving OCD a high five and saying, "Good call on the warning!"

When you avoid something because of OCD fears, several things happen:

1. You never learn that your fear may have been unfounded.
2. Your anxiety actually increases over time.
3. Your world gets smaller and smaller.
4. OCD gets rewarded and strengthened.

This applies to all OCD themes, whether you're avoiding:

- Certain words or numbers
  ("I can't say or think the number thirteen.")
- Specific thoughts or images
  ("I push away any thought about harm.")
- Places or situations
  ("I won't go to the hospital because of germs.")
- Making decisions
  ("I can't choose because what if it's wrong?")

- Particular objects
  ("I won't touch knives.")

- Relationships or intimacy
  ("I keep people at a distance so I won't harm them.")

Avoidance only makes OCD stronger. It's like trying to put out a fire with gasoline.

Take a moment to identify what you're avoiding because of OCD. Is there a person you won't talk to? A place you won't go? Words you won't say? Thoughts you won't let yourself think? Each of these avoidances is strengthening your OCD.

"It's not in my head . . . I can *feel* it!"

Sarah shifts uncomfortably in her seat. "Sometimes my skin literally feels contaminated," she tells me. "Like, I can feel the germs crawling on me. That can't just be in my head, right?"

"Actually, those sensations may be real," I tell her. "Your body is really creating those feelings. But they're responses to what your brain believes, not to actual danger."

This is one of the most confusing aspects of OCD. It creates powerful physical sensations that feel incredibly real. It's not just thoughts; you can literally feel contamination on your skin, an arousal sensation, a not-right feeling, or an overwhelming urge in your body.

Why does this happen? Brain scans show that OCD affects the parts of your brain that detect danger and process emotions. So when OCD is sending intrusive alarms, actual physical sensations follow.

These same sensations would be incredibly helpful if you were in actual danger. If you saw a bear while hiking, your racing heart, tight chest, and surge of adrenaline would help you react quickly. If you touched a hot stove, that burning sensation would make you pull your hand away instantly. If you ate spoiled food, feeling nauseated would stop you from eating more. Your body's warning system is designed to protect you; OCD just triggers it at the wrong times.

When your brain labels something as a threat, your body jumps into action. You might experience:

- Tingling or crawling sensations on your skin
- A sense of disgust or contamination
- Physical urges to perform compulsions
- Muscle tension or actual pain
- Stomach discomfort or nausea
- Sensations and arousal "down there"
- A feeling that something's "not right"

I want you to close your eyes (gotcha . . . now you can't read) and vividly imagine biting into a juicy, sour lemon. Really go for it—see the bright yellow skin as you slice it open.

Watch the juice drip down. Now take a big bite. Feel that intense sourness hitting your tongue, making your face scrunch up. Your mouth is watering right now, isn't it? Your taste buds are tingling, maybe you're even making that sour face?

"Is your mouth watering?" I ask Sarah.

"Yeah, it is," she says, surprised.

"Is there an actual lemon in your mouth?"

"No . . ."

That's how powerful the mind-body connection can be. Our brains will create a physical response to something that isn't actually there. That's exactly what happens with OCD.

The key insight here is that just because you feel it, that doesn't mean it's true. Physical sensations are powerful, but they're not always accurate indicators of reality.

The tricky part is that when you're trying *not* to feel a sensation, it practically makes you feel it. When you focus intensely on "I shouldn't feel anything in my groin" or "I shouldn't have a sensation on my skin," your attention zeroes in on exactly those areas, amplifying every tiny normal sensation until it feels significant. Your brain creates the very thing you're trying to avoid, the ultimate OCD trap.

Think about the physical sensations your OCD creates. Do you feel contaminated after touching certain things? Do you experience a "not right" sensation until you arrange things perfectly? An urge to confess or seek reassurance? These physical feelings are part of the OCD system, not evidence that your fears are justified.

Sneaky Compulsions That Keep You Stuck

Let's talk about one of the most important concepts for OCD recovery: sneaky compulsions.

Sneaky compulsions are the subtle, often invisible behaviors you engage in to reduce anxiety that don't look like obvious compulsions. They're especially tricky because they can fly under the radar, even when you think you're resisting OCD.

During our session, Sarah tells me, "I've been trying to cut back on the handwashing. But I noticed something weird. I find myself asking my roommate things like, 'Hey, did you have a friend over today?' "

"She thinks I'm just curious about her day, when in reality . . . if she had friends over, that means I'd have to clean all the knobs they potentially touched, avoid the couch, and reclean the bathroom. I'm being sneaky by asking a simple question."

Sneaky compulsions are OCD's backup plan. When Sarah resists the obvious ones, it offers alternatives that seem more reasonable or socially acceptable. Here are some common sneaky compulsions to watch for.

Telling your story (probably the biggest one): Repeatedly sharing an experience you've had to gauge reactions. Something like, "I stepped on these red spots that were on the ground while walking in the store."

You think it's blood—not just blood, but infectious blood. You're seeing if their reaction matches your brain's disaster scenario.

When they do not seem fazed by your experience, you add more details, thinking, "Maybe if they understood it better, they'd respond differently."

- This is reassurance-seeking, just more subtle.
- If they don't seem concerned, you feel better temporarily.

- It's a way to talk through it with someone to "figure it out," which keeps you stuck in the cycle.

Reassurance-seeking in disguise: Asking indirect questions to get confirmation that you're okay.

- "I saw this documentary about people who thought they were straight but were actually gay. (Instead of "Do you think I might be gay?")
- "I heard about this guy who snapped and hurt his family. . . . That's so weird, right?" (Instead of "You don't think I would ever snap, right?")
- "My friend told me they are struggling in their relationship. They watch a lot of TV together." (Instead of "We watch a lot of TV together. How's our relationship?")

Mental checking

- Replaying a conversation repeatedly in your mind, analyzing each word to make sure you didn't accidentally confess something terrible
- Replaying your morning routine to check if you locked the door, turned off appliances, or completed each step "correctly"
- Reviewing your thoughts during important moments to ensure you weren't having any "inappropriate" or "wrong" thoughts

- Reviewing a visit to a store, trying to recall if you put something in your pocket without paying
- Going through prayers or religious rituals in your head to check if you performed them correctly

Avoiding triggers: Subtly arranging your life to avoid facing your fears

- Taking the stairs instead of the elevator "for exercise" (really to avoid enclosed spaces)
- Only shopping online "for convenience" (to avoid touching items others have touched)
- Always being "too busy" to attend events (where your triggers might be present)
- Keeping the TV volume at an even number "because it sounds better"
- Asking someone else to handle knives "because you're clumsy" (when it's really harm OCD)

Self-monitoring: Constantly checking your own reactions and feelings

- Constantly assessing whether you feel "enough" love when looking at your partner
- Monitoring your groin responses during random daily activities to check for unwanted arousal
- Testing yourself by deliberately thinking of taboo topics to see if you feel disgusted "enough"

- Checking if you feel guilty "enough" after an intrusive thought about harm

Excessive research

- Googling, reading articles, or watching videos about your theme
- Reading this book . . . (Cough. Cough. Just kidding. You're in the right place.)

The problem with sneaky compulsions is that they keep the OCD cycle going just as much as obvious ones. They still reinforce the idea that your obsessions are important and dangerous.

The next time you feel anxious, pay attention to what you're doing to feel better. You might catch yourself doing sneaky compulsions you didn't even realize were compulsions.

Making Friends with Maybe

So far, we've talked about how OCD operates, the lies it tells, the way it creates physical sensations, and how it keeps you stuck through avoidance and sneaky compulsions.

But now I want to introduce a radical new way of thinking about all of this.

"Here's something to consider," I tell Sarah. "What if uncertainty isn't your enemy? What if it's actually the doorway to freedom?"

Sarah looks at me like I've suggested she should start eating rocks for breakfast.

"I know, I know," I laugh. "Right now, uncertainty feels

threatening. But what if you could learn to see it differently? What if uncertainty could actually be an okay thing? Maybe even a little exciting."

This is the beginning of a crucial mindset shift. OCD wants you to see uncertainty as a problem to solve. But what if it's just a normal part of the human experience?

Think about it: Many of life's most meaningful experiences involve uncertainty. New relationships. Creative projects. Adventures. Learning. Growth. All require stepping into the unknown.

"When you first learned to ride a bike," I ask Sarah, "did you have a hundred percent certainty you wouldn't fall?"

"No, of course not."

"But was it worth the uncertainty to learn how to ride?"

She nods.

"Living with OCD is like refusing to ride the bike unless someone can guarantee you'll never, ever fall. But that guarantee doesn't exist. And you miss out on the ride."

The problem isn't uncertainty itself. It's your brain's reaction to it. And that reaction can change.

I'm not saying this shift happens overnight. It's a gradual process of rewiring how your brain responds to the unknown. But it starts with creating a new relationship with uncertainty.

OCD's Playbook Exposed: Your First Assignment

Now it's time for your first real homework assignment. This isn't just busywork. It's the beginning of your treatment.

I pull out a worksheet titled "OCD's Playbook Exposed" and hand it to Sarah.

[Scan QR code.] →

"Your assignment this week is to write down everything you know about your OCD," I explain.

Sarah looks at the worksheet. "So I'm writing down . . . what, exactly?"

"Everything we just talked about," I tell her. "The lies, the justifications, the avoidance, the physical sensations, and those sneaky compulsions."

"How do I know when it's a lie?" Sarah asks.

"Well, if you even have to ask that question, it probably is," I say with a smile.

She can also look for these red flags:

- It demands certainty where none is possible.
- It uses extreme words like *always*, *never*, or *perfect*.
- It creates arbitrary rules you must follow "or else."
- It tells you that this time is different.
- It says feelings are facts.
- It insists on the importance of random thoughts.

I show Sarah some examples to get her started, like "If you don't check one more time, something terrible will happen" and "This physical sensation means your fear is real."

I want you, the reader, to fill out this worksheet too. Start by listing everything you can think of right now about your OCD.

Ask yourself:

1. What's the lie OCD is telling me right now?

2. What justification is it using to get me to do a compulsion?

3. What am I avoiding because of this fear?

4. What physical sensations am I experiencing?

5. What subtle compulsions am I doing?

This isn't just about identifying OCD's tactics. It's about creating distance. When you can say, "There goes OCD with its 'this time is different' justification again," you're already starting to break free.

"So, I'm becoming an OCD detective," Sarah says with a small smile.

"Exactly!" I tell her.

And that's what you'll be doing too. You're gathering evidence about how your OCD operates. Each lie, justification, and sneaky behavior you catch is another piece of evidence in your case. Once you've gathered enough evidence, you'll be ready to start building your defense against it.

In the next chapter, we'll dive deeper into the treatment process. We'll talk about motivation, goals, and how to create the right conditions for change. I'll set you up for success as you begin fighting back against OCD.

Chapter 3

Don't Get Caught Up in Your Theme

At our next session, Sarah looks confused when I tell her that her specific fear of germs doesn't really matter for treatment. Like most people with OCD, she finds this hard to believe. After all, she's been living with contamination fears for years, and now I'm telling her it's not about the germs?

I lean forward in my chair and share something crucial, something OCD doesn't want her to know. OCD wants everyone to think their specific theme and fear is the worst one. That it has deep meaning. That no one else experiences exactly what they're going through.

I can see recognition in Sarah's eyes as I explain that OCD wants her to believe her anxiety is special, uniquely terrible. But the truth is that the content, the story, the theme—they don't actually matter when it comes to treatment.

"That doesn't mean *you* don't matter," I quickly add. "It

means we're not going to keep paying attention to the story anymore. We're not going to analyze when it started or why you have these specific thoughts."

This is key. What *you* are thinking, reader, is valid. What you're feeling is valid. But the actual OCD content? That's just noise.

OCD is trying to convince you that what you're experiencing is super important. But our job in treatment is to teach your brain that maybe the specifics don't matter as much as it thinks they do.

The Many Faces of OCD

Let's take a quick tour through some common OCD themes. You might be thinking, "*Wait!* Didn't you just say themes aren't important? You'd be right. But what is important is your own identification with one or more of them.

As you read through these, you might have the thought, "That's exactly what I have!" or "Mine wasn't talked about . . . my OCD is unique." Or even "Wow, I wish I had that instead of what I'm dealing with."

That last thought? Classic OCD trap. More on that in a minute.

Checking OCD: The what-if machine. "What if I left the stove on and burn down the whole neighborhood?" "What if I didn't lock the door and someone breaks in?" "What if I left my wallet?" Check, check, and check again . . . and maybe one more time just to be safe. Then go back and check again anyway. You might be late to work because you had to drive back home three times to make sure the garage door is closed.

Contamination OCD: The poster child of OCD that everyone thinks they understand. "Those germs may get me sick." "What if I touch that doorknob and get my whole family sick?" Your hands are raw from washing, your house may smell like bleach, and you've got a mental map of every place people have been so you can clean afterward. You might have "safe" clothes for home and "contaminated" clothes for outside, or throw away perfectly good food because someone breathed near it. You use sanitizer, just because.

Disgust OCD: The extreme "ick" reaction. "This sensation is unbearable!" "I'll never feel clean again after touching that!" Unlike contamination OCD, which fears harm from germs, disgust OCD is about the overwhelming feeling of grossness itself. It can even come from a simple thought. You might avoid certain textures, smells, bodily functions, or situations that trigger intense disgust, even when you logically know they're harmless.

Emotional contamination OCD: The cousin of regular contamination, but with feelings instead of germs. "What if I catch that person's depression?" "What if their bad luck rubs off on me?" You might avoid certain people, objects they've touched, or places they've been, fearing their negative traits or bad fortune will somehow "infect" you.

Existential OCD: The reality questioner. "Is reality even real?" "What's the point of anything?" "What if we're living in a simulation?" "What if I don't actually exist?" Hours spent trying to solve puzzles that philosophers have debated for centuries, except you need an answer *right now* or you can't focus on anything else.

False memory OCD: The really bad time traveler. "Did I do something awful in the past that I can't remember clearly?" "What if I hit someone with my car and blocked it out?" "What if I actually molested someone but can't remember?" Then mentally rewinding and replaying fuzzy memories like a broken DVD skipping the same scene over and over again, trying to gain certainty about things that might never have happened.

Fear of losing control OCD: The "what if I snap?" worrier. "What if I suddenly scream in this quiet library?" "What if I jump off this balcony even though I don't want to?" "What if I just lose all impulse control?" "What if I acted out one of my thoughts?" You might avoid situations in which these intrusive thoughts occur, like quiet public places, certain people, or heights.

Harm OCD: Scary thoughts about hurting yourself or others. "What if I suddenly stab my spouse with this kitchen knife?" "What if I swerve into oncoming traffic on purpose?" "What if I lose control and hurt my child?" These terrifying thoughts invade your mind despite being the exact opposite of who you are. Your kitchen knives are hidden away, you take the long route to avoid driving over bridges, and you might ask your partner, "Do you think I'm a good person?" multiple times a day.

Health anxiety OCD: The WebMD spiral. "Is that headache actually a brain tumor?" "What if that twitch is the first sign of a deadly disease?" Every normal body sensation becomes proof of impending doom. You might doctor-shop for reassurance, constantly check your body for symptoms, or avoid learning about diseases because the information sends you into a spiral. You may avoid exercise or physical activity out of fear it may trigger symptoms.

Just right OCD: "It doesn't *feel* right yet." Tap, tap, turn, repeat until the magical "just right" feeling appears. You might rearrange objects until they feel balanced, reread sentences until they feel complete, or do actions in multiples until it feels "even." You might turn light switches on and off in patterns, rewrite text messages seventeen times, or get stuck in doorways because you didn't step through with the right foot first. It's not about being a perfectionist. It's about that maddening itch in your brain that won't go away until you feel "just right."

Memory hoarding OCD: The mental file cabinet. "What if I forget this important detail?" "I need to remember exactly how this conversation went." You mentally store excessive information, fearing that forgetting even small details could be catastrophic. You might take excessive photos, notes, or recordings to preserve memories that others would naturally let fade.

Pedophilia OCD (POCD): The theme that makes people feel a lot of shame. Unwanted thoughts about kids that lead to avoiding playgrounds, schools, or even family gatherings with children. You might be terrified of changing a diaper, bathing your child, or being alone with any minor because your brain keeps sending false danger signals about your intentions.

Perinatal/postpartum OCD: The terrified new parent. "What if I drop my baby?" "What if I snap and hurt my child?" "What if I'm a terrible parent?" Occurring during pregnancy or after childbirth, this theme attacks when you're most vulnerable and tired. You might avoid being alone with your baby, check them constantly, or seek endless reassurance about your parenting abilities.

Pure O (purely obsessional OCD): While Pure O isn't a specific theme, many people see it as its own thing. *Any of these themes can present as Pure O, meaning the compulsions are primarily mental rather than physical behaviors.*

You have intrusive thoughts but don't seem to do compulsions. In reality, you're doing tons of compulsions; they're just invisible. You might spend hours mentally reviewing, analyzing feelings, trying to cancel out "bad" thoughts with "good" ones, or asking yourself the same questions over and over. From the outside, you look fine but maybe just distracted. Inside, you're fighting an exhausting, hidden battle that no one can see.

Real event OCD: Guilt machine incoming. "What about that lie I told in third grade?" "Did I actually ruin my friend's life with that comment five years ago?" You dig up actual events from your past and put them under a moral microscope, transforming everyday mistakes into unforgivable sins. It can be in the distant past or a day ago. You might confess the same "crimes" repeatedly to different people to see their reaction, review old text messages for evidence of your horribleness, or apologize to someone for the twelfth time about something they barely remember.

Relationship OCD (ROCD): The relationship killer. "Do I

really love them?" "Is this really 'the one?'" "Why didn't I get butterflies when they walked in?" "What if I'm settling?" "Could I handle looking at that mole on their face forever?" You become a relationship detective, analyzing every tiny feeling, comparing your relationship to others, and asking for constant reassurance that you're with the right person.

Responsibility OCD: Everything falls on you. "What if I left a candle burning and the house burns down?" "What if someone trips on that pebble I didn't pick up?" Your brain has appointed you as the person who is personally responsible for preventing every possible disaster. You might triple-check the stove before leaving (and then drive back to check again), avoid recommending restaurants in case someone has a bad meal, or lie awake wondering if that email you sent might somehow cause your coworker to get fired.

Scrupulosity (moral) OCD: The ethics police. "What if I'm a fundamentally bad person?" "What if I'm contributing to harm by buying this product?" You hold yourself to impossible moral standards that no human could meet. You might ruminate for hours about whether you were rude to a cashier, obsessively research the ethical implications of everyday products, donate money you can't afford out of guilt, or constantly seek reassurance that you're a "good person."

Scrupulosity (religious) OCD: The spiritual failure. "What if God is mad at me for that thought?" "Did I pray wrong?" "What if I sinned by accident when I yawned?" Your faith, which should bring you peace, instead makes you scared all the time. You might say the same prayer over and over until it feels "right," confess things you've already confessed, skip church because you're afraid of having bad thoughts there, or create special rituals to make sure God isn't upset with you.

Sexual orientation OCD (SO-OCD): Figuring out who you are. "Did I just find that person attractive?" "What if my entire sexual identity is a lie?" "Why did I notice their hair—does that mean something?" "Did I feel aroused when I saw them?" Your brain turns normal human observations into evidence that you need to question yourself. You might avoid movies with attractive actors of certain genders, mentally "test" your reactions when you see people, analyze your past relationships for "clues." The most frustrating part? The more you try to gain certainty about your orientation, the more doubt your brain creates.

Somatic (sensorimotor) OCD: The body hyperawareness trap. "Am I breathing right?" "Why am I so aware of my blinking?" "Why can't I stop noticing my swallowing?" Once you notice a normal bodily function, you can't stop focusing on it, creating a cycle of anxiety about something that should happen automatically. Or maybe it's the opposite: You notice breathing on purpose out of fear that if you don't, you may stop breathing. You might avoid activities that make you aware of these sensations or keep yourself busy to distract yourself from the sensations.

Suicidal OCD: "What if I did it?" "What if I actually want to die?" "What if I can't trust myself around bridges or pills?" Unlike genuine suicidal ideation, you're terrified of these thoughts and desperately don't want to act on them. You might avoid tall buildings, medications, or sharp objects, fearing not that you want to die, but that you might somehow lose control.

Superstitious/magical thinking OCD: The invisible cause-and-effect believer. "If I don't tap three times, someone I love will get hurt." "If I think a bad thought and don't remove it, it might come true." You do things to try to stop bad stuff from happening, like avoiding the number thirteen, or tapping four times before you enter a room. These actions have nothing to do with preventing bad things, but your brain tells you they do.

There are many more ways people might identify with a theme.

But they're all OCD.

And no matter what anyone tells you, there's no such thing as a "better" or "worse" OCD theme. The theme that feels worst to you is whichever one you're currently experiencing.

Why You Have *Your* Specific Theme

"But why contamination?" Sarah asks. "Why am I so scared of germs specifically?"

You might be wondering the same thing. Why *your* specific theme?

Here's the answer, and it's actually pretty simple: OCD attacks what you value most.

Think about it. Got relationship OCD? You probably really value having a loving, good relationship. Harm OCD? You're probably a really safe, kind person who would never hurt anyone. POCD? You value kids' safety big time.

Look at your own theme for a second. What's it targeting? I bet it's something you deeply care about.

"That makes sense," Sarah says, nodding. "I've always

been super careful about health and worried about my family getting sick."

Exactly. OCD doesn't pick random themes. It goes after what matters most to you. It's like a missile locked onto your core values.

Why Treatment Doesn't Care What Theme You Have

"I don't get it," Sarah says. "If my OCD attacks what I value most, how can the theme not matter?"

I bet you're wondering the same thing.

When I run groups for OCD, I often hear someone say, "Wow, I wish I had their theme instead of mine. Theirs seems easier to deal with."

Have you ever felt that way? Like someone else's OCD would be easier to handle than yours?

The grass is always greener on the other side.

But here's the truth: If you had what they had, you'd feel exactly the same way. Because underneath all these different themes is the same core issue. Can you guess?

Uncertainty.

Think about it. Are you actually afraid of something you know for sure? Or are you afraid of something you're uncertain about?

"I'm afraid I might get sick," Sarah says. "But I don't know if I will or not."

This is true for you too. Take a moment and think about your obsessions. Aren't they all about things you can't be 100 percent certain about?

This is the case for 99 percent of OCD themes. (You'll notice I didn't say 100 percent. I like to leave that uncertainty there.) The real fear is uncertainty.

When OCD Changes Masks

Another reason not to get too caught up in your specific theme? It might pack its bags and a new theme might move in next month.

"Wait, what?" Sarah asks. "My germ fears might just . . . go away?"

"Not exactly," I explain, chuckling. "OCD is like that annoying friend who keeps changing their personality based on whatever show they just binged."

Most people with OCD may experience a few different themes throughout their life. Life changes like getting married, having a baby, or starting a new job can trigger these switches. But sometimes they change just because OCD got bored with the old theme.

As our values change, so can OCD.

"So today I'm terrified of germs, but next week I might suddenly start worrying if I'm a good person?" Sarah asks.

"Exactly!" I tell her. "And here's what's even wilder: sometimes you don't even trade one theme for another. You can actually collect them, like Pokémon cards. I've worked with people who started with contamination fears, then added in relationship doubts, then sprinkled on some harm thoughts, all running at the same time."

Sarah laughs, but then her expression changes. Her eyes dart to the side and she shifts uncomfortably in her chair.

"Actually . . ." she starts, then stops, like she's afraid to continue.

"What is it?" I ask gently.

She takes a deep breath. "It's funny you mention that. The contamination stuff is still there, but lately . . . I've been having these other thoughts too." Her voice drops to almost a whisper. "Really scary ones."

"Tell me about them," I encourage her.

"Last week, I was making dinner. I picked up a knife to cut vegetables, and out of nowhere, I had this vivid thought about . . . about stabbing my kids." Her eyes fill with tears. "It was so clear in my mind. I dropped the knife and ran out of the kitchen. I've been ordering takeout all week because I'm terrified to cook now."

She looks up at me, desperate. "What kind of mother even thinks that? I love my children more than anything in the world. I would never hurt them. Never! But these thoughts keep coming, and they feel so real. My husband thinks I'm just tired, but I'm actually terrified I might . . . do something."

I nod, completely unsurprised. (My lack of surprise always surprises my clients!)

"And how do these thoughts make you feel?"

"Horrified!" she exclaims. "Disgusted. Scared. Like the worst mother on the planet. These aren't thoughts I want to have. They feel like they're being forced on me."

"Exactly," I tell her. "And that's actually a really important point. These thoughts are ego dystonic, which means they go against everything you believe and value. Real dangerous people don't worry about being dangerous. They don't feel disgusted by these thoughts. The fact that you're so upset by them is actually evidence that they're just OCD."

Hold up, reader. . . . Do you see what I just did there? I just gave Sarah some reassurance. This isn't something I do lightly.

Typically, in the beginning stages of educating yourself about OCD, it can be important to understand that OCD thoughts, feelings, and urges are *ego dystonic*, meaning they do not align with your values, your goals, or who you are as a person. This is why it causes so much distress. It's like the brain insisting you like blue cheese when you know you don't and have never liked it.

However, once you learn and understand this concept, it's important not to get stuck there. During treatment, it's not your job to keep proving to yourself that these thoughts are ego dystonic. Constantly analyzing whether thoughts align with your "true self" or seeking evidence that you're "really" a good person becomes its own form of reassurance-seeking, another compulsion that keeps you trapped in the OCD cycle.

The goal shifts from "proving" these thoughts don't represent you to accepting that thoughts are just thoughts, regardless of their content.

For Sarah it may feel very real. With the contamination, she knew it was probably excessive. But these thoughts . . . they're so vivid, and OCD is using one of its favorite phrases: "This one is different."

Now, I need to be clear about something before we continue. What I'm about to ask you isn't meant to provide reassurance. I don't want you to use this as another compulsion, checking and rechecking your answer. This question is meant to help you see a bigger pattern, to provide enlightenment rather than temporary relief:

Has your OCD ever been right before?

All those times you were convinced something terrible would happen if you didn't perform your compulsion. All those hours spent checking, washing, avoiding, or mentally reviewing. All those times you were absolutely certain danger was imminent.

How many times did the disaster actually happen?

I'm guessing almost zero, but I run into those people who say, "But mine actually came true! I did leave the stove on." And I ask, "So what happened?" and the answer is almost always . . . nothing.

The catastrophe in your head tends to be a lot worse than what actually happens.

Your OCD might switch from contamination to harm, from relationship doubts to moral scrupulosity, but it's using the same old playbook. Same doubt, same uncertainty, different costume.

You might be wondering, "Why would my brain do this to me? I'm already dealing with one kind of OCD. Why would it give me another? Especially one that feels so much worse?"

But is it really worse? Or does it just feel that way because it's targeting something else you deeply value?

This mask-switching habit of OCD is exactly why getting stuck on the content is pointless. You're chasing the mask, not dealing with what's underneath. The real problem isn't which mask OCD is wearing today—it's the same OCD underneath, running the same old tricks in your brain.

It's like your brain is using an outdated operating system. Probably Windows 95.

I share this comparison with Sarah, and it gets a small smile from her. Sometimes a little humor helps us see our OCD for what it really is: outdated programming that's desperately in need of an upgrade.

Then Why Even Talk About Themes?

"If the theme doesn't matter," Sarah asks, "why did we just spend so much time talking about all the different types?"

Great question. Here's why:

People need to feel heard and understood. When you've been struggling with terrifying thoughts about harming your child or constant doubts about your relationship, you need someone to acknowledge what you're going through.

Talking about themes helps you recognize that:

1. You're not alone and others experience similar thoughts.
2. These thoughts don't define you—they're just OCD.
3. Your specific fear makes sense given what you value.
4. Your OCD has a name and is recognized.

But while understanding your theme helps you feel validated, it's not what helps you get better.

That's why in my office, we might spend some time talking about your theme, but then we pivot to treating the OCD itself, not the specific content.

When Your Theme Becomes a Trap

There's a real danger in getting too caught up in your theme, and OCD knows this. It wants you to think your theme is special, is unique, and requires special treatment.

I want you to listen closely. Right now, your OCD is probably whispering (or maybe shouting) that your situation is the exception to the rule. I've heard thousands of variations of this same argument.

Many people tell me, "My theme has real risk." This is one of OCD's favorite tricks. It convinces you that while other people's OCD might be irrational, yours is the exception. Yours is based on a real danger that you must keep monitoring.

I hear these excuses all the time:

"Sure, but there is a lot of flu going around."

"Yeah, but this is my eternal salvation. Everyone else is risking temporary things, mine is eternity."

"But I actually live in a high-crime area. That's why I check the door so many times."

What's your OCD's favorite excuse? Can you spot it when it shows up?

Sarah jumps in, "But having violent thoughts about my

kids feels different than worrying about germs. These are my children and I'm supposed to protect them!"

I nod. "I understand. And that's exactly what OCD wants you to think . . . that your theme is the special one that deserves extra attention and caution. But everyone with OCD feels this way about their theme. Everyone believes their fear is the 'reasonable' one."

When you focus too much on your theme, you:

1. Get stuck analyzing the content instead of treating the process

2. Waste time trying to "solve" the obsession (which is impossible)

3. Miss the common patterns that all OCD follows

4. Make recovery harder by believing your OCD is *special*

I've seen people spend years trying to figure out why they have certain themes or trying to analyze their way out of their obsessions. It doesn't work. Ever.

You Matter . . . Your Theme Does Not

Here's what you need to understand. *You* matter. Your well-being matters. Your relationships matter. But the specific content of your OCD? It's just noise in your head trying to get your attention. Like a toddler having a tantrum in the grocery store, the more attention you give it, the louder it gets.

Identifying your OCD is only step one. Naming it doesn't fix it. It's the action part that makes all the difference, and don't worry—we're getting there soon.

Think of it like spotting a fire in your kitchen. Saying "That's a fire!" doesn't put it out. But you can't grab the fire extinguisher if you don't first recognize what you're dealing with.

In the next chapter, we'll grab that extinguisher. We'll talk about why understanding OCD isn't enough, and I'll teach you exactly what methods to use when your brain starts sending those false alarms.

Chapter 4

We Can't Just Talk About It

Let me guess . . . at this point, you're thinking, "Great, I understand my OCD now. Problem solved!"

Not so fast.

Understanding OCD is just the starting point. Knowing how an engine works doesn't make you a mechanic. You need tools, skills, and most important, you need to actually get your hands dirty (in more ways than one).

Many of my clients come to their first session expecting therapy to look like it does on TV. You know the scene: soft lighting, soothing music, talking about childhood while having profound realizations. The therapist nods sympathetically and says, "And how does that make you feel?"

But effective OCD treatment looks nothing like that.

Why Talking Isn't Enough

Here's an uncomfortable truth: You can't talk your way out of OCD.

You could spend years discussing your contamination fears, harm thoughts, or relationship doubts. You could analyze when they started, why you have them, and how they make you feel. You could gain incredible insights about yourself.

And you'd still be stuck doing compulsions.

Because with OCD, insight isn't enough.

Think about it. When you talk extensively about your OCD worries, what happens? You get reassurance that feels good for a minute. You analyze the thought, turning it over and over. You try to find meaning in it.

And that only strengthens OCD's grip.

The talking approach fails for several reasons:

1. **It gives meaning to OCD content.** When you spend hours analyzing why you have certain thoughts or fears, you're telling your brain, "These thoughts are important and worth examining." But OCD thoughts aren't meaningful; they're just noise.

2. **Analysis leads to more analysis.** You can't think your way out of OCD. The more you analyze, the deeper into the rabbit hole you go.

3. **Talking provides temporary relief.** Discussing

your fears with a sympathetic person feels good momentarily, but it's really just a form of reassurance. And like all reassurance, it doesn't last.

4. **Words don't change behavior.** Knowing intellectually that your fears are excessive won't stop you from acting on them when anxiety spikes.

This is why so many people spend years in traditional talk therapy and still struggle with OCD. They're applying the wrong treatment approach to a condition that requires action.

ERP: The Treatment That Actually Works

So, if talking doesn't work, what does? The answer is Exposure and Response Prevention (ERP).

I know, I know—just the word *exposure* probably makes your stomach tighten. But stick with me, because this is the most effective treatment we have for OCD, and we're going to dive deep into exactly how it works in the next chapter.

Here's the basic idea: You deliberately face your fears while refusing to do the compulsions that typically follow. It sounds simple, but it's incredibly powerful because it breaks the cycle that keeps OCD alive.

For someone with contamination OCD, this might mean touching a doorknob and then *not* washing your hands afterward. For relationship OCD, it might mean having doubts about your partner and not seeking reassurance or checking your feelings.

"But that sounds terrible!" you might be thinking. "When I don't do my compulsions, my anxiety gets worse!"

Exactly, in the short term. But what happens in the long term when you keep doing compulsions? The fear comes back. And you have to do the compulsion again. And again. And again.

Doing compulsions sends a message to your brain that there really was danger and that the compulsion saved you. ERP breaks that cycle.

Your Brain Learns Through Experience, Not Talk

Here's the science behind why ERP works when talking doesn't: Your brain learns through experience, not discussion.

I often tell my clients, "It's like learning to drive. You can study the driver's manual, watch driving tutorials, and understand every traffic rule perfectly. But until you actually get behind the wheel and practice, you won't become a driver."

When you do an exposure and then resist compulsions, several important things happen in your brain:

1. **You build evidence that contradicts your fears.** Your brain sees that anxiety subsides naturally, even without doing compulsions.

2. **You develop tolerance for uncertainty.** You practice living with "maybe" instead of demanding certainty. Most life experiences are in the maybe zone already; we just need to learn to embrace it.

3. **You experience habituation.** Through repeated exposure, your brain gets bored of the trigger and stops sending false alarms.

4. **You build confidence in your ability to handle anxiety.** Each successful exposure proves you're stronger than you thought.

This experiential learning rewires your brain in ways that talking simply cannot.

Think of getting into a hot tub. It could feel like it's almost unbearable; your body might be screaming at you to get out. But after a bit, your body adapts. It doesn't feel as hot as it did at first. In fact, you may even feel like you want to be hotter.

Ding. Ding. Ding. Your brain learned something new about a situation because you experienced it.

What Real OCD Treatment Looks Like

Let me be clear about what effective OCD treatment is: It's active. It's challenging. Sometimes it's uncomfortable. But it works.

Instead of just talking, you'll:

- Identify your triggers and compulsions.
- Create a hierarchy of exposures, from easier to more challenging.
- Gradually work through fears, learning that you can handle anxiety and resist doing compulsions.
- Track your progress and adjust as needed.

And yes, there is some talking involved. But it's focused on planning exposures, problem-solving obstacles, and celebrating progress. Not endlessly analyzing thoughts or fears.

ERP *Is* Difficult

Let's address the elephant in the room: ERP is hard. It's probably one of the hardest things you'll ever do.

Many therapists minimize this, so eager to get clients to try ERP that they downplay the difficulty. But I've always found honesty works better.

The difficulty of ERP isn't in the exposures themselves. It's in the response prevention—the willingness to feel uncomfortable without doing anything to fix it.

It's about sitting with uncertainty and anxiety, learning that you can handle these feelings without doing compulsions. It's about discovering that feelings, no matter how intense, will eventually pass on their own if you let them.

But here's the good news: You don't have to do it perfectly. You just need to be willing to try. Not perfection, but a commitment to keep showing up, even when it's uncomfortable.

And you won't be doing it alone. Whether you're working with a therapist or using this book as your guide, you'll have support along the way.

Getting Ready for Action

At this point, you're probably feeling a mix of emotions.

There's fear: "Can I really face my biggest fears on purpose?" There's doubt: "Will this actually work for me?" There's resistance: "This sounds way harder than just talking." And somewhere underneath, there's hope: "Maybe I could finally be free."

All these reactions are normal. Expected, even. ERP isn't easy, but neither is living with OCD.

So, here's what I need from you: commitment. Not perfection, but a willingness to try even when it's uncomfortable. Can you give me that?

In the next chapter, I'll show you *exactly* how ERP works its magic. You'll discover how this powerful treatment physically rewires your brain, creating new neural pathways that can finally quiet the relentless obsessions and anxiety.

And don't worry, I already know that voice in your head is probably listing a dozen reasons why ERP won't work for you specifically. That nagging voice might be suggesting hypnosis, meditation, or some miracle supplement instead. That resistance? It's not just normal but is actually part of OCD's survival strategy.

Chapter 5

The Magic of ERP

Picture this: There's a big red button sitting right in front of you.

Above it, a sign warns: "DANGER: If you don't press this button, someone you love might get hurt."

Now, the button isn't real (obviously). But that little jolt you just felt? That urge to press the button? That's 100 percent real.

What if I told you that the path to beating OCD involves looking at that button, letting the urge wash over you *without* pressing it, and then walking away without checking to make sure everything's okay?

Welcome to Exposure and Response Prevention. It's the most effective OCD treatment out there, and the one thing your OCD will fight like crazy to keep you from doing.

I've watched thousands of people turn their lives around with ERP. People who spent hours stuck in rituals now living freely. People who couldn't escape scary thoughts now barely noticing them. People who swore their OCD was different or too severe now managing it like pros.

ERP isn't rocket science. The theory of it is actually super simple. But in practice? It takes guts. It takes showing up consistently. And it means being willing to feel uncomfortable now for freedom later.

Let's check back in on Sarah, who has just walked through my office door.

"Sorry I'm late," she says, dropping into the chair across from me. Her hands are still red and raw, but something in her eyes has changed. "I almost didn't come back."

"What stopped you? I mean, you completely ghosted us in chapter four."

She laughed. "I kept thinking there had to be another way to fix this. I went down an internet rabbit hole looking into hypnosis, EMDR, and even acupuncture."

"Ah yes, the classic OCD detour," I chuckled. "Your OCD will suggest literally anything else besides the one thing that actually works."

Sarah settled in, looking both nervous and determined. "Okay, I'm ready. No more distractions. Tell me about this ERP magic."

What the Heck Is ERP, Anyway?

Let's break down what ERP actually is. You've probably heard the term tossed around, but what does it really mean?

As I've mentioned, ERP stands for Exposure and Response Prevention. Let's break it down.

Exposure: This is where you deliberately face the stuff that triggers your OCD. Yeah, on purpose! You're basically walking straight toward the things your brain is screaming at you to avoid.

This could be:

- Being around things your OCD says are dangerous (like knives in the kitchen or being alone with loved ones)
- Writing out those horrible thoughts your OCD makes you avoid thinking
- Creating those body sensations that freak you out (like feeling short of breath or dizzy)

Response Prevention: This is the harder part. After you trigger your OCD, you *don't* do the rituals your brain is begging you to do. When anxiety kicks in, you resist the urge to perform compulsions, seek reassurance, or escape.

This means stopping:

- Physical stuff like washing, checking, or arranging things
- Mental tricks like reviewing memories, counting, or "canceling out" thoughts
- Avoiding places or situations that trigger you
- Asking people if you're okay or googling your fears

Here's the key difference between ERP and just "facing your fears": With regular exposure therapy (like for a fear of spiders), you face the fear until you calm down. But with OCD, the goal isn't to feel better right away. It's learning to live with not knowing for sure. You sit with the discomfort without doing anything to "fix" it.

The magic happens when these two parts work together. Exposure without response prevention is just torture. You face your fears but then you end up feeding the OCD with compulsions. Response prevention without exposure doesn't teach your brain anything new.

That's it! No complicated theories. Just facing your fears and choosing not to do the stuff that keeps OCD alive.

"That sounds . . . terrifying," Sarah admitted, sinking deeper into her chair.

"It can be," I said, nodding. "But you know what's more terrifying? Spending the next twenty years trapped in OCD rituals."

Here's how ERP works in real life. When you do an exposure, you're basically telling your brain, "Hey, I know you think this is dangerous, but I'm gonna do it anyway."

Then, when you prevent the response (the compulsion), you're saying, "And I'm not doing the safety behaviors you think I need. I'm just gonna sit with this uncertainty."

Let me show you what I mean. Picture two different paths your brain can take when OCD shows up.

The first one is the path most people with OCD know all too well, the one that keeps you stuck.

By facing your fear and resisting compulsions, you create a new learning experience for your brain, a new pathway that retrains the faulty signals sent by OCD.

I imagine OCD saying to itself, "Huh, I told this person

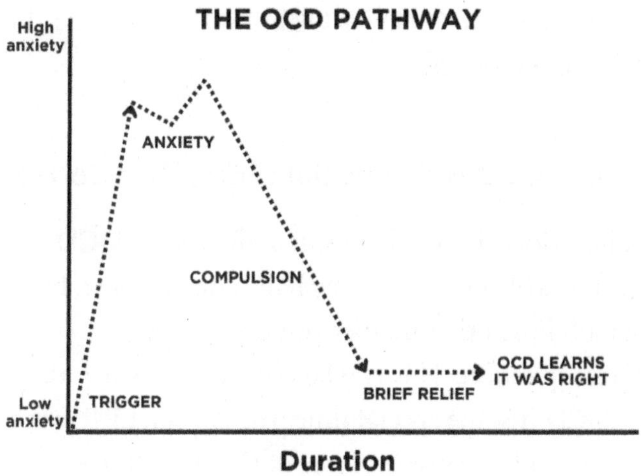

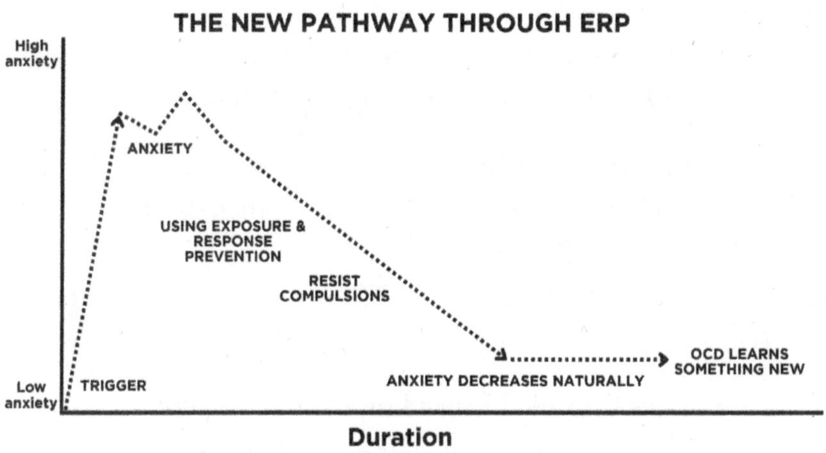

they were in danger. They didn't do what I told them would keep them safe and yet their anxiety seemed to drop anyway. Also, they don't appear to be reacting as if they are in danger. . . . Maybe I need to stop warning them so much."

This is the *new* behavior OCD learns when you do not listen to its demands.

Your OCD Isn't Special (Sorry, Not Sorry)

"But how does this work for different types of OCD?" Sarah asks. "I mean, not washing my hands makes sense, but what about all those other themes you talked about?"

Great question. This is where people get stuck thinking their OCD is some special unicorn. But the ERP process is the same no matter what flavor of OCD you have.

Check it out:

FOR CONTAMINATION OCD

- *Exposure:* Touch doorknobs, use public bathrooms, handle "contaminated" stuff.
- *Response Prevention:* Don't wash hands after, don't use sanitizer, don't change clothes, don't ask if you'll be okay.

FOR HARM OCD

- *Exposure:* Hold kitchen knives, be alone with loved ones, write out your scary thoughts.
- *Response Prevention:* Don't avoid triggers, don't mentally review to make sure you didn't hurt anyone, don't seek reassurance.

FOR RELATIONSHIP OCD

- *Exposure:* Look at attractive people who aren't your partner, notice when you don't feel "in love," watch sappy romance movies.
- *Response Prevention:* Don't compare your relationship to others, don't check your feelings, don't ask others if you seem happy together.

FOR RELIGIOUS SCRUPULOSITY

- *Exposure:* Write out "blasphemous" thoughts, do normal activities on religious days, make small mistakes in religious practices.
- *Response Prevention:* Don't pray to "cancel out" thoughts, don't confess repeatedly, don't seek reassurance from religious leaders.

"So, it's the same basic idea no matter what theme you're dealing with," Sarah says, the light bulb going on.

"Exactly!" I replied. "The content, what your OCD focuses on, might be different, but the process is identical. You expose yourself to uncertainty and you don't try to fix it."

My Brain on ERP: How It Actually Changes Things

"But how does this actually work in my brain?" Sarah says. "Because right now, my brain feels totally broken."

"Not broken," I tell her. "Just stuck in some bad habits. But here's the cool thing about your brain—it can change."

Let me tell you about something called neuroplasticity. Don't worry about the fancy word. It just means your brain can create new pathways throughout your life. Your brain isn't set in stone. It's constantly changing based on what you do.

When you have OCD, certain paths in your brain have become superhighways. The route from trigger to compulsion is like a well-traveled road with no speed limits or stop signs.

But the good news is that you can build new roads.

Each time you do an exposure without performing compulsions, you're carving out a new path. You're teaching your brain, "See? This isn't actually dangerous. We faced it and nothing terrible happened." (And yes, OCD may whisper, *But what about next time?*)

The first few times, it's like hacking through a dense jungle with a dull pocket knife. It's tough work. The path isn't clear. But each time you travel that route, it gets a bit easier. The path gets wider.

Eventually, that new pathway, the one that says, "Uncertainty is no big deal," becomes your brain's preferred route. The old OCD superhighway gets less traffic. It doesn't disappear completely, but it becomes more like an abandoned dirt road than a major interstate.

This is what happens in your brain when you practice ERP:

1. Your brain's alarm system chills out and stops freaking out over OCD triggers.

2. Your brain's "logical mind" gets better at spotting false alarms.

3. Your body produces fewer stress chemicals when faced with uncertainty.

4. New brain connections form, creating healthier thought patterns.

"So I'm literally rewiring my brain?" Sarah asks, looking both impressed and skeptical.

"Absolutely." I nod. "We can actually see these changes on brain scans. People who successfully do ERP show different brain activity than before. The parts that were overactive with OCD become calmer."

And the best part? These changes stick around. They're not just temporary fixes. You're building new mental hardware, not just running a quick software update.

Why Feeling Anxious During ERP Is Actually Good

Here's something that might sound backward: For ERP to work, you usually need to feel some discomfort, like anxiety or uncertainty, during the exposure.

I see you there, closing this book, thinking, "I'm out!"

Keep reading, because it may be the piece you're missing in your recovery.

Think of it like exercise. If you're lifting weights and it feels totally easy, are your muscles getting stronger? Nope.

There needs to be some resistance, some challenge, for growth to happen.

Same with ERP. If, when you do an exposure, you feel completely calm, your brain isn't learning anything new. It's just confirming what it already knows. This isn't a very good exposure!

It only knows what you teach it.

This is a crucial point that many people miss. It's tempting to do exposures while distracting yourself, using breathing techniques, or getting reassurance to keep your anxiety low. But that defeats the whole purpose.

The magic of ERP happens when:

1. You feel the anxiety spike during an exposure

2. You *don't* do anything to artificially lower that anxiety

3. You stay in the situation long enough for your brain to learn that:

    - Anxiety doesn't last forever.

    - Bad things don't happen just because you think they might.

    - You can handle uncomfortable feelings without fixing them.

    - If you run into a real problem, you can solve it.

"So . . ." you might be wondering. "I'm supposed to just . . . feel terrible and do nothing?"

Not exactly. You're feeling the anxiety and just noticing it rather than fighting it. You're saying, "This feels awful, and I'm going to stay here anyway." It's like watching a scary movie. The goal isn't to get rid of anxiety, but to change how you react to it.

This shift doesn't happen overnight. But with practice, your brain starts to file anxiety under "annoying but not dangerous" instead of "EMERGENCY: DO SOMETHING NOW!"

What to Say When OCD Is Screaming

When you're in the middle of an exposure and your anxiety is climbing, what should you actually say to yourself? This is where response statements come in. These are verbal tools that help you resist compulsions and sit with uncertainty. There are two main types that work really well:

1. Embracing Uncertainty

Instead of seeking certainty (which is what OCD wants), you purposely admit that you can't know for sure. A few examples of what this might look like:

- "Maybe these thoughts do mean something about me, maybe they don't. I'm cool with not knowing."
- "Perhaps I did leave the stove on. I'm choosing to live with that possibility."

- "I don't know if this doorknob has germs on it or not, and that's fine."
- "Maybe I'll get sick, maybe I won't."

2. Agreeing with the Threat

This technique sounds weird, but it's super powerful. Instead of arguing with your OCD (which never works), you actually agree with the possibility.

Examples:

- "Maybe I will harm someone I love. If that happens, I'll deal with it then."
- "Yes, I hope this is contaminated and I get terribly sick. Bring it on."
- "I'm totally in the wrong relationship and it's awesome."

These statements aren't about believing the worst will happen. They're about showing your brain that even that possibility isn't so scary you need to avoid it.

The trick is saying these with a casual, even bored, tone, as though you're talking about what you might have for lunch. This teaches your brain that these thoughts aren't emergencies.

Notice how different this is from what OCD wants. OCD demands certainty, promises safety through rituals, and catastrophizes the unknown. Your response statements do the opposite. They welcome uncertainty, reject false safety, and treat the unknown as boring rather than catastrophic.

When you first try these statements, they'll feel deeply uncomfortable. That's the point! With practice, they become more natural, and eventually, you'll find yourself responding to OCD with a mental shrug instead of panic.

Your Brain Doesn't Want You to Do ERP

Here's where things get interesting. Your brain is about to throw everything it has at you to avoid doing this treatment. You know why? Because if you do it, OCD loses its power, and it really doesn't want to give that up.

OCD gets super creative when it comes to avoiding treatment.

Here are just a few of the things your brain will tell you:

"This isn't the right time to start."

There's that big project at work, your kid's school play, the holidays coming up . . . There's always a reason to delay. But guess what. There's never a perfect time to start ERP. The best time is now.

"There has got to be another way."

OCD loves suggesting alternatives to ERP because it knows ERP actually works. Don't fall for it. Those other methods might help with general anxiety, but they won't fix OCD.

"You're doing it wrong."

Your brain will try to convince you that you're not doing ERP correctly, so why bother? Remember: Imperfect ERP is still effective.

"This is making you more anxious, so it must be bad."

Increased anxiety during exposure is actually a sign it's working! Just like feeling sore after a workout, this is part of getting stronger.

"Your OCD is too severe for ERP."

Classic excuse. There's no such thing as OCD that's too severe for ERP. More severe OCD just means you might need more support or a more gradual approach.

"You don't really have OCD."

When all else fails, OCD will try to convince you that you don't even have OCD, and that you're just actually dangerous, contaminated, evil, or whatever. This is a desperate last attempt to avoid treatment.

Sarah nods vigorously. "I've definitely told myself all of these things! Especially the 'this isn't the right time' one."

"Everyone does," I say. "Being aware of these excuses is

half the battle. When you hear them pop up, you can say, 'Nice try, OCD, but I'm doing ERP anyway.'"

ERP: Can I Do This Alone?

"Can I really do this by myself?" you might be wondering. "Or do I need a therapist to guide me through every step?"

ERP can absolutely be done independently, and many people successfully reduce their OCD symptoms using self-directed approaches. But working with an OCD specialist has some significant advantages:

1. The specialist can help design effective exposures tailored to your specific fears.
2. They provide accountability when OCD tries to derail your progress.
3. They can spot subtle compulsions you might miss.
4. They offer support and encouragement when you feel discouraged.
5. They can adjust the approach based on how you respond.

Consider working with a professional if:

- Your OCD is severe and significantly impacting your daily functioning

- You've tried self-directed ERP without success
- You have safety-related obsessions that feel genuinely risky
- You're dealing with other mental health conditions like depression or trauma
- You feel overwhelmed by the prospect of facing your fears alone

The ERP Timeline

Everyone wants to know: "How long until I feel better?"

I'm always hesitant to promise any specific timeline. Instead, I use the cliché . . . "Everyone is different and it depends."

I'll try to give you a rough overview here, but do not get caught up in it. Maybe it takes you more time. Maybe less. Just do the work and see what happens.

Weeks 1–2: Building courage. This is the toughest part because you're feeling more anxious as you face your fears, but you're developing the crucial skill of sitting with discomfort. You're learning that anxiety doesn't kill you. Small win: You're finally doing something different from the endless OCD cycle.

Weeks 3–4: Reclaiming small freedoms. Those easier exposures start requiring less effort. You'll find yourself not thinking about certain triggers that used to grab all your attention. You're getting back minutes of your day that OCD used to steal.

Weeks 5–8: Expanding your world. You're now handling situations that once seemed impossible. Your confidence grows as you see yourself doing things you couldn't imagine doing before. Friends and family might notice you seem less distracted or tense.

Months 3–6: Taking back your life. The majority of people experience substantial symptom reduction by this point. You're spending way less time on OCD behaviors and more time on things you value. Your brain is creating new, healthier pathways.

Beyond 6 months: Living, not just surviving. OCD becomes more background noise than the main soundtrack of your life. You have tools to handle setbacks. You know how to recognize and address OCD when it pops up, but it's not controlling your decisions anymore.

Here's something else to remember: Progress isn't a straight line. You'll have good days and bad days. That's normal. The overall trend is what matters, not any single day.

Think of it like weight loss. The scale might bounce up and down daily, but over weeks and months, the trend line moves in the direction you're aiming for. Some days OCD will feel stronger, maybe because you're stressed, tired, or going through other stuff. Other days, you'll barely notice it. These ups and downs don't mean treatment isn't working; they mean you're human.

As I write this, I can think of many people who've seen major relief from symptoms in even a week of really going hard with ERP. This tells you that the frequency and commitment of doing ERP really can make a difference.

But Am I Actually Going to Do It?

I can explain ERP all I want, and most clients I see might be willing to *try* it. But I find they haven't really bought into it. If I rush the process, we don't see the results we're hoping for. And even though it pains me not to jump straight to what's going to make you better, there's one last step before we can start ERP.

Can you guess what it is?

You need to convince yourself that this treatment is worth your time, energy, and anxiety.

Doing ERP is like climbing a mountain. The techniques we've talked about are your gear—essential, but not enough on their own. Before you start climbing, you need to know why you're making the journey in the first place.

Without strong motivation, most people quit ERP when it gets uncomfortable. And it will get uncomfortable. So, before we dive into the actual exposures, we need to build a rock-solid foundation for your recovery.

Because here's the real secret to ERP: It works when you have a good reason to stick with it.

When you can see exactly what OCD has taken from you and what you want back, you'll find the strength to do the hard work.

In the next chapter, we'll figure out your personal why: the reason that will keep you going when things get tough.

Chapter 6

Finding Your Why

In all the years I've been working with people with OCD, I've noticed a pattern. They may understand the OCD cycle. They can explain uncertainty. They even identify their sneaky compulsions. But when it comes time to actually do something about it, they hesitate.

And honestly? That makes perfect sense. I mean, who in their right mind eagerly volunteers to face their worst fears on purpose?

Before we dive into the nuts and bolts of ERP, before we create your hierarchy and design your first exposures, we need to address the most important question of all. . . .

Why would you put yourself through this?

Building Your Foundation

I always start by asking patients a simple but powerful question:

"What has OCD cost you?"

This question cuts right to the heart of things. We need

to be honest about what OCD has stolen from your life. Not to make you feel bad, but to light a fire under you for the work ahead.

I want you to grab a pen and paper right now. Seriously, don't just read over this part. Actually write this down. What has OCD cost you? Make a list of everything OCD has stolen from your life.

[Scan QR code.] →

Let me share just a few of the things I've heard from patients:

- "Two hours every morning just checking everything before I can leave."
- "My relationships—I keep pushing people away when they get too close."
- "My college education—I dropped out because I couldn't focus."
- "My presence with my family—I'm physically there but mentally gone."
- "Sleep—I lie awake analyzing conversations for hours."
- "My confidence—I feel broken and hopeless."
- "My marriage—my partner is walking on eggshells around me."
- "My career growth—I'm too afraid to take on new responsibilities."

- "Money—on therapies that didn't work and replacing clothes and food that I didn't need."
- "My spiritual peace—constant doubts about being a good person."
- "My religion—I can't read my scriptures, because I'm having blasphemous thoughts."
- "My time—hours focusing on bodily sensations and unable to think clearly."

Sarah looked at her own list. She had written about hours lost to handwashing and how she'd stopped cooking for her family because of frightening thoughts about knives. As she read through it, her expression changed completely.

"It's a lot to see on paper, isn't it?" I said quietly. "OCD doesn't just take small things—it takes big chunks of your life. Your time with loved ones. Your career opportunities. Your peace of mind. Your freedom to do simple things others take for granted."

The "Building Your Foundation" worksheet will help you uncover exactly what OCD has cost you. The more honest and specific you can be, the stronger your motivation will become for recovery.

This isn't meant to depress you. It's meant to make you angry. Not at yourself, but at OCD. Because OCD is a thief. It's been robbing you for too long, and that anger might just be the thing that motivates change.

Your Reason for Change

This is the point where many people say they understand what OCD has taken from them, but that doesn't make facing their fears any easier.

They're right—but understanding the cost gives them a reason to face their fears anyway.

This is the critical difference between people who succeed in OCD treatment and those who don't. It's not about how severe your OCD is or how long you've had it. It's about having a "why" that's stronger than your fear.

In the worksheet provided, you'll clarify your personal reasons for taking on this challenge. Think carefully about who you're doing this for (hopefully yourself, first and foremost) and what you hope to gain.

What's your why? What goal or dream is worth going through the discomfort of treatment? What would you fight for, even when it gets tough?

As you think and write your answers, here are some common whys I've heard from others:

- "I want to be present for my family instead of trapped in my head."
- "I refuse to let OCD steal another decade of my life."
- "I want to be able to travel and experience the world."
- "I'm tired of living a half-life, always controlled by my fears."

- "I want to actually enjoy my relationship instead of questioning it constantly."

Your why needs to be compelling enough to sustain you through the hard parts of treatment. It needs to be something you can hold on to when OCD is screaming at you to do your compulsions.

So . . . what's yours? Write it down. Make it specific. Make it emotional. Make it powerful.

The Brutal Truth About Motivation

Here's something they don't tell you in most recovery books: Motivation is fickle. It's here one day, gone the next.

"Some days I wake up ready to fight this thing," clients tell me. "And other days I just want to give in to every compulsion because it's easier."

That's completely normal. Nobody feels motivated all the time. I have a gym membership that can verify this fact.

This is why relying on motivation alone is a recipe for failure. You'll have days when you feel ready to conquer the world, and days when getting out of bed feels impossible. OCD knows this, and it will happily wait for your motivation to wane before striking hard. It's like going grocery shopping on an empty stomach: You may leave the store with more than you intended.

Instead, we need to develop commitment: a promise to act regardless of how you feel in the moment.

If you decided to start running every morning, there would definitely be days when you woke up and didn't feel like running. It's raining, you're tired, your bed is comfy. But if you only ran when you felt motivated, you'd barely run at all.

The same is true for fighting OCD. There will be days when ERP feels impossible. Days when giving in to compulsions seems like the easier choice. This is when commitment, not motivation, will carry you through.

This doesn't mean you should beat yourself up when your motivation dips. It just means you need a more reliable system than "feeling like it." You need structures that keep you moving forward even when motivation is low.

Getting Support for the Journey

I've seen countless clients try to battle OCD alone. They decide no more checking or no more reassurance-seeking and then give up by lunchtime.

"That's like trying to climb Mount Everest without a guide," I tell them. "Technically possible, but why make it harder than it already is?"

Recovery from OCD is tough enough with support. Without it, the odds drop dramatically. You need people in your corner who understand what you're facing and can help hold you accountable. These people might be:

- A therapist trained in ERP (ideal, but not the only option)
- A support group (in-person or online)
- A trusted friend or family member

- An OCD book with structured exercises (like this one!)

I've seen the huge difference support makes. Remember Sarah? When her OCD shifted from handwashing to scary thoughts about knives, her husband stepped up big-time. She was clear with him: "Don't tell me I'm a good mom when I ask. And when I avoid cooking, gently encourage me to try anyway." With that guidance, he became her teammate instead of accidentally feeding her OCD. He learned when to push, when to back off, and how to help without enabling.

Who can be your support person? Who in your life would be willing to learn about OCD and help you stay committed to your recovery? Write down their name.

If you truly don't have anyone in your life who can fill this role right now, that's okay. Online support groups can be incredibly helpful. Organizations like the International OCD Foundation have resources and community forums where you can connect with others who understand exactly what you're going through.

The key is not to try to do this alone. OCD thrives in isolation. It wants you to think you're the only one struggling, that no one else would understand. This is just another lie.

Getting Specific: What Do You Want Back?

"I know what OCD has taken from me," clients often say. "But to be honest, I've been living this way for so long, I'm not even sure what life without OCD would look like."

This hesitation is more common than you might think. When you've been stuck in the OCD cycle for years, it can be hard to imagine a different kind of life. Your goals might feel vague: "be less anxious" or "stop obsessing."

But vague goals lead to vague actions. We need specifics!

Here's something that helps a lot of my clients: Sit down and honestly weigh your options.

On one side, you've got treatment. Yeah, it's tough and uncomfortable. You'll have to give up those safety behaviors that feel so necessary right now. It's like jumping out of a plane with a parachute. Logically you know it'll work, but your brain still screams, "BAD IDEA!"

On the other side, you've got staying exactly where you are. Sure, it feels familiar. You know what to expect. The problem? You'll just get more of the same: more time lost, more opportunities missed, more life unlived.

In the worksheet, you'll find a section that walks you through this decision. Most people eventually realize that the scariest option isn't treatment. It's letting OCD keep calling the shots for another five, ten, or twenty years.

"If OCD wasn't running the show," I like to ask, "what would you do differently tomorrow? What would your morning look like?"

Some may say, "I'd check my email once, not twenty times to make sure I didn't accidentally write something offensive. I'd make a decision about what to wear without second-guessing if it 'means' something about my identity. I'd text that person I've been interested in, instead of analyzing whether I'm 'certain enough' that I like them."

Now, *these* are specific goals. They paint a picture of what recovery looks like in practical, everyday terms.

Your turn. Write down what your life would look like without OCD controlling it. Be specific about what you would do differently. What activities would you engage in? What places would you go? What conversations would you have?

Don't just write "I'd be happy" or "I'd be less anxious." Write actual, observable behaviors that would change:

- I would leave the house in less than ten minutes.
- I would use public bathrooms when needed.
- I would say "I love you" without analyzing if I meant it enough.
- I would let my child play at the playground without constantly watching for dangers.
- I would make decisions without seeking reassurance.
- I would cook meals using knives no matter who's around me.

These specific goals give us targets to aim for. They help us design exposures that are directly relevant to the life you want, not just generic "face your fears" exercises.

The Power of Tracking

During one of my sessions with Sarah, when we'd finished discussing her why, I leaned forward and said, "Sarah, there's one more piece we need before we dive into ERP. We need to know exactly what we're dealing with."

She looked confused. "But I already know what my OCD makes me do. I wrote them all down earlier, remember?"

"Yes," I said, nodding, "but we need more detail. We need to track the specific triggers, the thoughts your brain attaches to them, and the compulsions you do in response. This gives us a map of your OCD. Without this map, we'd be treating OCD blindfolded."

For the next week, I want you to become an OCD detective. Carry a small notebook or use your phone to record every time OCD shows up, or use the provided worksheet.

[Scan QR code.] →

You're going to catch it in the act, when you're triggered or after you've done a compulsion. Here's what I want you to notice:

1. The trigger: What set it off?
2. The obsession: What meaning did your brain put on it?
3. Your anxiety level: 0–10, with 10 being the highest
4. The compulsion: What did you do to reduce anxiety?

Here are some examples of tracking logs:

Trigger: *Noticed I didn't feel butterflies when my partner walked in*

Obsession: *"What if I don't really love them? What if I'm settling?"*

Anxiety: 7/10

Compulsion: *Mentally reviewed our relationship history, looked at old photos to check my feelings, asked friend if their relationship has ups and downs*

Trigger: *Knife in kitchen drawer*

Obsession: *"What if I lose control and hurt someone? What kind of person thinks these thoughts?"*

Anxiety: 9/10

Compulsion: *Put knife in back of drawer, ordered takeout instead of cooking, avoided being alone with family members*

Trigger: *Touched doorknob at mall*

Obsession: *"There could be dangerous germs that might make me sick."*

Anxiety: 8/10

Compulsion: *Used hand sanitizer 4 times, kept hands away from face, washed for 15 minutes when got home*

This tracking serves several important purposes:

1. It makes you more aware of the OCD cycle as it's happening.

2. It shows you patterns you might not have noticed.

3. It clearly shows your main compulsions.

4. It gives us specific material to work with for ERP.

Most important, tracking helps you see that OCD follows a predictable pattern. It's not random, and it's not as powerful as it wants you to think. It's a broken record, playing the same fears over and over, even if the *content* of those fears changes, like when Sarah's moved from contamination fears to harm thoughts involving her children.

Your Rock:
The One Thing That Matters Most

As my session with Sarah is drawing to a close, I ask her one final question.

"Sarah, out of everything we've talked about today, including the costs of OCD, your why, your support person, and your specific goals, what's the one thing you'll hold on to when ERP gets tough? What will be your rock?"

She thought for a moment, twisting the tissue in her hands. "My kids," she said finally, her voice growing stronger. "Being able to cook dinner for them again even with these horrible thoughts. Being fully present for bedtime stories instead of being stuck in my head worrying about germs or harm." She looked up, determination in her eyes. "That's my rock—being the mom I want to be, not the mom OCD forces me to be."

In the worksheet, you'll find a place to record your personal statement: something that will remind you to continue treatment even when you're feeling hopeless. This is your rock. Write it down, take a picture of it, make it your phone background, do whatever helps you keep it front and center when things get tough.

What's your rock? What one image, goal, or promise to yourself will you cling to when OCD seems too strong to fight? Make it specific and emotional. This is the fuel that will drive your recovery when motivation fades.

Ready or Not, Who Cares?

"I still don't feel completely ready," Sarah admitted during one of our sessions.

"You don't have to be," I told her. "Nobody ever feels a hundred percent ready to face their biggest fears. But you're committed. That's what matters."

You don't start ERP because you feel ready. You start because you're committed to the life you want on the other side of fear. You start because you've had enough of what OCD has taken from you. You start because even though the path looks terrifying, staying stuck looks worse.

My challenge to you as we close this chapter:

1. Complete your OCD cost list. Be brutally honest.
2. Write down your why, the reason that makes recovery worth the discomfort.
3. Identify at least one support person or resource.
4. Track your OCD for the next week using the format I showed you.
5. Define your rock: the one image or goal you'll return to when things get tough.

Take time this week to work through the "Building Your Foundation" worksheet. Fill it out completely, even if some questions feel difficult or uncomfortable. This isn't just busywork. It's the foundation that will support you through treatment.

Writing these out may feel like an exposure itself, but remember, when you're facing a fear, your brain is getting stronger.

In the next chapter, we'll use all this to build your ERP plan. We'll create a hierarchy of fears, design your first exposures, and start the real work of recovery.

You don't have to feel completely ready. You just have to be willing to take the first step.

Chapter 7

Exposure

Today's session is different. Instead of meeting in person, I'm doing a virtual session with Sarah as she practices an exposure in her own kitchen. I've found that exposures done at home seem more real than those in an office setting. "I know I need to face my fears, but I'm not sure I can do this," Sarah says, staring at the kitchen knife on the counter. Her hands are clenched tight at her sides, and she's standing at what she probably considers a safe distance—about five feet away.

"That makes total sense," I tell her. "If you weren't scared, we wouldn't need to do this work."

Sarah's eyes dart between me and the knife. Her breath is quick and shallow. "I can't stop picturing it. What if I lose control? What if I grab it and—"

I gently cut her off. "Let's not feed that story right now. Remember what we talked about? All the fluff your brain is throwing out doesn't matter. What matters is your willingness to feel uncomfortable without doing compulsions."

She nods, but I can see the doubt in her eyes. And I get

it. We've been building up to this moment for weeks. We've worked through understanding OCD, identifying compulsions, and finding her why. Now it's time for the part that actually changes everything: exposure.

And let's be honest: This is the part most people dread. If you're reading this chapter with a knot in your stomach, you're not alone. Exposure work is hard. It's uncomfortable. And it's also the most powerful tool we have for breaking free from OCD.

What Is Exposure, Really?

Before we dive in, let's get crystal clear on what exposure actually is (and isn't).

Exposure is deliberately facing the things that trigger your OCD fears while choosing not to do compulsions in response. That's it.

Here's what exposure is *not*:

- It's not about testing whether your fears come true (spoiler: anything is possible).
- It's not about "proving" your OCD wrong through logical debate.
- It's not about eliminating anxiety completely.
- It's not about white-knuckling through panic until it passes.

Instead, exposure is about changing your relationship with uncertainty and anxiety. It's about teaching your brain, through direct experience, that you can handle the discomfort of not knowing for sure.

Think of it like learning to swim. You can read books about swimming techniques, watch YouTube videos of Olympic swimmers, and listen to podcasts about the psychology of swimming. But until you actually get in the water, you won't learn to swim.

Exposure is getting in the water.

Yes . . . There Are Some Ground Rules

Before we dive into the fun stuff, let's establish some nonnegotiable ground rules. (Don't worry, they're pretty reasonable.)

Rule 1: We don't do anything to hurt ourselves or others. Exposure is about facing fears, not creating actual danger. Your brain may scream that you're "going too far," but we're going to trust your internal instincts to kick in when there's real danger.

Rule 2: We don't do anything illegal. This might seem obvious, but it's worth stating: Exposures never involve breaking laws. If your OCD involves fears about breaking laws, we'll work with imaginal exposures instead or do things that make you feel like you're breaking the law.

Rule 3: We don't actually violate your core values (even though it'll feel like it). OCD loves to attack your deepest values, so exposures might feel like they're crossing moral lines. They're not. We design exposures that help you face uncertainty while staying true to who you actually are.

With these boundaries in place, let's learn about the different types of exposures and how to actually do them.

The Three Flavors of Exposure

Not all exposures look the same. Depending on what triggers your OCD, you'll need different approaches. Think of these as different tools in your toolbox:

1. In Vivo Exposure (the "Real World" Approach)

"In vivo" is fancy talk for "in real life." These are exposures in which you directly face the actual things, places, or situations that trigger your OCD in the real world. It's "hands-on" exposure.

For example:

- If you're afraid of germs on doorknobs, you actually touch a doorknob.
- If you avoid the kitchen because of knife fears, you go into the kitchen.
- If you avoid certain words or numbers, you say or write them out.
- If you fear driving over bridges, you drive over an actual bridge.

In vivo exposures are usually the most powerful because they provide direct, real-world experience that your brain can't easily dismiss. They're like telling your brain, "Look, I'm doing the thing you're afraid of, so now what?" (I'm imagining your brain wearing a shocked Pikachu face right now.)

For Sarah, this means actually being in the kitchen while knives are present, not just thinking about it or looking at pictures of knives. She'll start by just being in the same room, then progress to watching someone else use knives, and eventually to holding and using them herself.

2. Interoceptive Exposure (the "Body Sensations" Approach)

"Interoceptive" refers to sensations inside your body. These exposures involve deliberately creating the physical feelings that trigger your OCD.

Sometimes it's not the doorknob that triggers your OCD—it's the sweaty palms you get after touching it. Or it's not the knife itself, but the tension you feel in your arms when holding it. Maybe it's the dizzy feeling you don't like or your heart rate going up.

In these exposures, you:

- Create those uncomfortable body sensations on purpose.
- Sit with the discomfort without doing compulsions.
- Learn that the sensations aren't as scary as your brain thinks.

Some examples:

- If dizziness triggers panic, you might spin in a chair for thirty seconds.

- If your heart racing scares you, you might jog in place or climb stairs quickly.
- If certain sensations in your groin area cause anxiety, you might practice sitting and standing quickly to create minor sensations.
- If feeling your breathing makes you anxious, you might deliberately pay attention to your breath.

For Sarah, this might mean purposely creating tension in her arms (the sensation she gets when holding knives) and not doing anything to make the feeling go away. This teaches her brain that the sensation itself isn't dangerous, even if it's uncomfortable.

3. Imaginal Exposure (the What-If Approach)

Imaginal exposures happen in your *imagination*. (Thanks for that insight, Captain Obvious.) Think of them as what-if scenarios that you purposely play out in your mind to practice tolerating uncertainty.

These are perfect for situations in which you can't (or definitely shouldn't) create the actual scenario in real life:

- You can't and shouldn't create a situation in which you will harm someone.
- You can't go back in time to check if you hit someone with your car.
- You can't know for certain if you made the "right" choice about your relationship.

With imaginal exposure, you:

- Write or record detailed scripts about your feared scenarios (as if they're happening right now).
- Include lots of uncertainty in these scripts ("maybe it happened, maybe it didn't").
- Listen to or read these scripts repeatedly while preventing compulsions.
- Practice sitting with the anxiety without seeking reassurance.

It's like telling your brain, "Let's imagine the very thing you're afraid of and practice handling the uncertainty around it."

For Sarah, this means writing out detailed scripts about her feared scenarios with knives. Not because these scenarios are likely to happen, but because facing the uncertainty about them helps break OCD's power.

Finding Your Core Fear (Time to Play Detective)

Here's where most people mess up their exposures. They focus on the surface-level stuff instead of digging deeper to find what they're really afraid of.

How do you find *your* core fear? Try this "downward arrow" exercise:

[Scan QR code.] →

1. Write down your specific OCD fear or trigger.

2. Ask yourself: "What would it mean if this fear came true?"

3. Look at your answer and ask again: "And what would *that* mean?"

4. Keep digging deeper with "And what would *that* mean?" until you hit bedrock.

Let me show you how this works with a real example. Meet Tom, who has responsibility OCD:

Tom's surface fear: "I need to check that my email to my boss didn't have any mistakes."

Me: "What would it mean if there were mistakes in the email?"

Tom: "My boss might think I'm careless."

Me: "And what would *that* mean, if you were careless?"

Tom: "She might give me a poor performance review."

Me: "And what would *that* mean, if you got a poor review?"

Tom: "I could lose my job."

Me: "And what would *that* mean, if you lost your job?"

Tom: "I wouldn't be able to support my family."

Me: "And what would *that* mean, if you couldn't support your family?"

Tom: "I would be responsible for my family's suffering. I would be a failure as a provider and a disappointment."

Bingo! Now we've hit the core fear. It's not really about the email, it's about the fear of being responsible for something bad happening to people Tom cares about.

Once Tom sees this, he realizes his checking compulsions aren't just about emails. They show up when he drives (checking rearview mirrors repeatedly), when he cooks (checking food temperatures obsessively), and even in conversations (mentally reviewing everything he said to make sure he didn't offend anyone).

All these seemingly different behaviors are driven by the same core fear. And that means he can design exposures that target this fear across different situations.

Choosing the Right Tool for the Job

Each type of exposure has its place, and most recovery plans use all three. But how do you decide which to start with?

Start with in vivo whenever possible. If your fear can be directly faced in real life without causing actual harm, start there. In vivo exposures tend to be the most powerful because they provide direct evidence that you can handle the uncertainty.

Use interoceptive when physical sensations are key triggers. If your OCD is triggered by bodily sensations like breathing awareness, heart rate, or feelings that aren't "just right," interoceptive exposure directly addresses these triggers.

Use imaginal for situations that can't be directly created. If your fears involve harming others, catastrophic scenarios, or situations that can't be ethically or practically simulated, imaginal exposure is your go-to.

Most effective treatment plans use a combination. For example, Sarah's plan includes:

- In vivo: Being in the kitchen with knives, eventually holding and using them
- Interoceptive: Creating tension in her arms and the "urge" she fears
- Imaginal: Writing scripts about her worst fears coming true

Still, Sarah is wary. "If I write out my feared thoughts," she asks, "isn't that just feeding them? Won't that make them stronger?"

This is one of the most common misconceptions about exposure. Writing out your fears doesn't make them more likely to happen (but maybe it does . . . for you reassurance seekers). It doesn't put the idea in your head, because it's already there, throwing a party and refusing to leave. What it does is help you practice tolerating the discomfort of those thoughts without engaging in compulsions.

Remember, the goal isn't to eliminate the thoughts, it's to change your relationship with them.

What a Complete Exposure Actually Looks Like

Before we jump into creating exposures, we need to understand what a full exposure involves from start to finish.

Without this understanding, you might create a great list but not know how to actually do them effectively.

A complete exposure has several essential pieces:

1. **Clear identification of the trigger.** What exactly are you exposing yourself to? Be specific. "Touching a doorknob" is much clearer than "facing contamination fears."

2. **Duration.** How long will you stay with the exposure? Until your anxiety reduces by half? For ten minutes? Until you're bored?

3. **Response prevention plan.** Which compulsions will you resist during the exposure? Make a specific plan for each one.

4. **Response statements.** What will you say to yourself when anxiety rises? Prepare these in advance. (We'll dive deep into this in the next chapter.)

5. **Anxiety tracking.** How will you monitor your anxiety during the exposure? Usually I recommend rating it from 0 to 10 at regular intervals.

6. **Repetition schedule.** How often will you repeat this exposure? Daily? Multiple times per day? What's your consistency plan?

An example:

- **Trigger:** Touch the bathroom doorknob at work.
- **Duration:** Maintain contact for thirty seconds, then don't wash hands until next meal.
- **Response prevention:** No handwashing, no sanitizer, no asking for reassurance, no mental review of germ facts.
- **Response statements:** "Maybe I'll get sick, maybe I won't. In fact, I sure hope I do."
- **Anxiety tracking:** Rate your anxiety on a scale of 0 to 10 every few minutes, continuing until either your anxiety level drops by half or you feel ready to stop. Keep in mind that reduced anxiety isn't always the best indicator that you're finished with the process; there's more nuance to consider, which we'll explore later on.
- **Repetition:** Do this eight times at work every day.

Let's Create an Exposure Together

Let's walk through creating one complete exposure using Sarah's situation. Now, typically you'd build a full hierarchy before starting any exposures, and we'll cover that process later. But right now, I want to focus on something equally important: learning how to design one solid exposure from start to finish.

Think of this as learning the blueprint for a single room before we design the entire house. In chapter 10, you'll build your complete hierarchy, but understanding how to create one well-designed exposure will make that process much clearer.

First, let's play a quick game. Based on what you know about Sarah's knife fears, can you guess what her core fear might be? Take a moment to think about it.

Got your guess? Let's see if you're right!

We'll use the downward arrow technique with Sarah:

Surface fear: "I might use a knife to hurt my children."

Me: "What would that mean if it happened?"

Sarah: "It would mean I harmed the people I love most."

Me: "And what would that mean?"

Sarah: "It would mean I'm a dangerous person."

Me: "And what would that mean?"

Sarah: "It would mean I'm not the person I thought I was. I'm actually a monster pretending to be a good mother."

Me: "And what would that mean?"

Sarah: "It would mean my entire identity is a lie. I've been fooling everyone, including myself."

Sarah's core fear: Being a bad person (specifically, being a monster disguised as a loving mother).

Did you guess correctly? If so, you're getting really good at understanding how OCD works!

Now here's where things get interesting. Once we understand that Sarah's core fear is about her identity as a good person, we can design exposures that directly target this fear, not just the surface trigger of knives.

Designing the Exposure

For Sarah's core fear of "being a bad person/monster disguised as a loving mother," we might consider having her:

- Be alone with her children (in vivo)
- Write scripts about possibly deceiving herself about who she really is (imaginal)
- Create tension in her arms while holding a knife and saying, "Maybe I am a monster. Maybe I'm not." (combination)

Notice how these target her core fear, not just the superficial fear of knives. This makes them much more powerful.

After discussion, Sarah decides to start with: "Holding a chef's knife while sitting next to my husband, who is preparing dinner."

Sarah rates this as a 5 out of 10 on her anxiety scale. It's the perfect middle ground—not so low that it won't activate OCD, and not so high that it feels overwhelming. You might be surprised that holding a knife doesn't raise her anxiety to a 10, but everyone is different, and your goal is to challenge yourself. Not every exposure has to start with the *smallest* step you can think of.

The one thing to look out for is picking an exposure that you can repeat. Her exposure is good, and it's something she can actually do. However, with an exposure like this, she has to wait twenty-four hours to do it again. So, let's see if we can change it a bit.

Making It Specific

Sarah decides: "I will hold the chef's knife in the kitchen and stand at the counter where I normally prepare food, holding the knife in a natural cooking position."

You'll note that she has set clear parameters she can follow and track. This can be done at any time of the day and multiple times a day.

Identifying Potential Compulsions

Sarah lists what she might be tempted to do:

- Mentally reassuring herself ("I would never hurt anyone because I'm a good person.")
- Asking her husband for validation ("You don't think I'm a bad person, right?")
- Holding the knife awkwardly so as to be careful
- Distracting herself by looking at her phone
- Leaving the room if her anxiety gets too high

Planning Response Prevention

For each potential compulsion, Sarah creates a specific plan:

- Instead of mental reassurance: "When I catch myself trying to prove I'm good, I'll say, 'Maybe I am a monster in disguise. No one can know for sure.' "
- Instead of asking for reassurance: "I won't ask my husband anything about my character."

- Instead of avoiding: "I'll grip the knife harder when I feel like being extra careful."
- Instead of distraction: "I'll keep my phone in another room and focus on the uncertainty."
- Instead of leaving: "I'll commit to staying as long as it takes while embracing the doubt about who I really am."

Notice how Sarah's responses now target her core fear about her identity, not just her surface-level fear about knives.

Preparing Response Statements

Sarah writes down statements for when anxiety arises:

- "I'll never know with 100 percent certainty what kind of person I truly am deep down."
- "Maybe, maybe not."
- "How fun that I can keep such an amazing secret from everyone."

Wait, hold up. . . . Sarah is saying what? Yes, you read that last one right. Think about how much power gets taken away from OCD when you simply agree with it. (We'll talk about this more in the next chapter.)

Creating a Tracking System

Sarah plans to rate her anxiety every five minutes (there is no magic number):

- Starting anxiety level
- 5 minutes in
- 10 minutes in
- 15 minutes in
- Final anxiety level after 20 minutes

Planning for Repetition

Sarah plans to repeat this exact exposure at least five times daily over the next week before moving to something more challenging.

Some people prefer to really master one specific exposure before moving on, repeating the same scenario daily until it becomes second nature. Others like to mix it up, working on several different exposures simultaneously to keep their brain on its toes.

The key is finding an approach that challenges you consistently without overwhelming you completely. Sarah's single daily exposure is a solid start, but scaling up the frequency could accelerate her progress significantly.

With this detailed plan, Sarah knows exactly what she'll be doing, how she'll prevent compulsions, and how she'll track progress. This is a well-designed exposure: specific, measurable, and armed with strategies for response prevention. After Sarah completes this multiple times and gets comfortable with it, she'll be ready for something slightly more challenging.

But what if her anxiety doesn't decrease? That's okay too. Reduced anxiety isn't the measure of success. If it doesn't go down, don't worry—your brain is still learning something really important.

What your brain is actually learning when anxiety stays high: that you can function even when you feel terrible. You're showing that anxiety isn't dangerous, just uncomfortable. Sometimes the most powerful exposures are the ones where anxiety stays high but you choose to stay present and continue through life anyway. We'll dive deeper into how to tell if treatment is actually working in chapter 11, but for now, know that progress isn't always about feeling better—sometimes it's about getting better at feeling.

Okay, okay . . . I know I'm trying to sound clever. But what I want you to know is this: You get to choose and live in peace, happiness, and freedom. Anxiety doesn't get a vote and doesn't matter as much as we think.

Writing Scripts for Imaginal Exposure

For imaginal exposures, writing a script is often the most effective approach. Here's how to create one that works:

[Scan QR code.] →

Focus on Your Core Fear

I know, I keep harping on the core fear. But it's crucial that you're exposing yourself to the right thing.

Write in First Person, Present Tense

"I am holding the knife. My children are playing nearby. I feel the weight of the knife in my hand. I might lose control."

This makes it more vivid and immediate. Notice how I didn't write about actually harming someone? Your brain is already throwing out the worst-case scenarios—you don't have to.

Include Uncertainty

This is crucial. Don't write an ending in which everything turns out fine. Instead, embrace the uncertainty: "Maybe I will lose control. Maybe I won't. I can't know for sure."

Include Physical Sensations and Emotions

"My heart is racing. My palms are sweaty (mom's spaghetti). I feel terrified." These details make the script more emotionally activating.

Keep It Manageable

Aim for one to two paragraphs at most. You'll be reading this repeatedly, so keep it manageable.

Here's a snippet of what Sarah's script might look like:

I'm standing in the kitchen making dinner. My kids are playing in the next room. I can hear their laughter. I pick up the large chef's knife to cut vegetables. The knife feels heavy in my hand. My heart starts racing. I'm having thoughts about walking into the next room. My palms are sweaty. My chest feels tight. I feel like I've been fooling myself all along. Deep down, I'm not the loving mother I pretend to be. There's a monster hiding inside me that no one can see, not even me. Maybe I am, maybe I'm not. I can't know for sure. I choose to live with this uncertainty about who I truly am deep down, and continue making dinner without checking, without avoiding, without seeking reassurance.

"This feels awful to write," Sarah admits after working on her script. "It's like I'm inviting the thoughts in."

"The thoughts are already there," I remind her. "You're just facing them head-on instead of running from them. And that's incredibly brave."

Different Ways to Use Your Script

There are multiple ways to work with an exposure script:

Read it repeatedly. Practice responses like "Yep, could happen" and "Maybe, maybe not" while focusing on relaxed body language.

Record and listen. Record it with normal inflection, like you're reading an audiobook, not in a scary monotone.

Write it over and over. Sometimes the act of writing it repeatedly can be powerful.

Get creative. Record it into a voice changer or song-creation app. This takes away its power by turning something serious into something kind of silly. Can you imagine listening to your worst fears set to music? It transforms terror into absurdity.

When you get bored of the script, add more triggering details or create a new story.

The Reality of Exposure Work

Exposure work is messier than any book can describe. You'll have days when your anxiety barely drops. Days when you catch yourself doing sneaky compulsions halfway through. Days when you feel like you're making no progress.

That's normal. This isn't about perfection, it's about *practice*.

The goal isn't to do perfect exposures; it's to consistently practice facing uncertainty without compulsions.

Sarah's journey wasn't a straight line. After her kitchen exposure, she had days when she felt more confident, followed by setbacks when her anxiety spiked again. Sometimes she caught herself doing subtle compulsions, while at other times she was able to fully embrace the uncertainty.

But each exposure, perfect or not, was a step forward. Each time she chose to face her fear instead of running from it, she was rewiring her brain's response to uncertainty.

Common Challenges (and How to Handle Them)

When you start doing exposures, OCD is going to try really hard to make you doubt your treatment. Here are some common thoughts that'll pop up:

"My anxiety isn't decreasing during exposures. It's not working." This happens! What matters is the learning that happens and the cumulative effect over time. If anxiety is reduced, great. If it isn't, also great. You're just going with the flow.

"I feel worse after starting exposures." This is common at the beginning. When you stop avoiding and start facing fears, you might temporarily feel more anxious. Think of it as cleaning out an infected wound: It might sting more at first, but it's part of the healing process.

"I'm not sure if I'm doing this right." Ask yourself: Am I fully facing the trigger? Am I preventing compulsions? Am I using helpful response statements? If you're answering yes, you're on the right track. If you're still questioning, sometimes the best answer is "Maybe, maybe not" and then doing it anyway.

"My OCD theme changed after I started exposures." This is OCD's sneaky way of trying to escape treatment. When you make progress with one theme, OCD might throw a new fear at you. The approach remains the same: Face the uncertainty without compulsions. Keep doing exposures for the original fear too; it will show you how little that fear mattered to begin with.

"I did exposures but my anxiety came back." Recovery isn't linear. You'll have good days and bad days. The overall trend is what matters, not any single day.

Preparing for the Other Half: Response

Throughout this chapter, we've focused on the *E* in ERP—Exposure. We've explored the three types of exposures, how to design them effectively, and what a complete exposure looks like from start to finish. But exposure is only half the equation.

The *RP* in ERP—Response Prevention—is equally critical. In fact, doing exposures without the right response strategy is like building a car with no engine. You've got the structure, but you're missing the power that makes it work.

That's why the next chapter is so crucial. We'll dive deep into exactly what to say to your OCD when it starts throwing thoughts at you, and how to prevent those sneaky compulsions that keep you stuck.

Chapter 8

Response

Now that you've learned how to create exposures, you're probably eager to jump right in. But the next part, the response, is where the real magic happens.

Exposure alone isn't enough. You could expose yourself to every trigger on your list, but if you're still responding to OCD the same way you always have, you won't see lasting change. It's like buying healthier groceries but still deep-frying everything.

What you do *after* the triggering thought appears is actually more important than the exposure itself. This is where most people get stuck and, honestly, where the biggest breakthroughs happen.

Think of it this way: You and OCD are like two people having a conversation. OCD has been saying outrageous things, and you've been arguing back, trying to prove it wrong. But what if you just . . . stopped arguing? What if you responded in a way OCD never expected?

That's what we're about to learn.

The Difference Between Being Exposed and Doing an Exposure

During a recent session, Sarah looked frustrated after trying her knife exposure at home. She had managed to stay in the kitchen, hold the knife briefly, and resist her usual compulsions, but she wasn't seeing the results she hoped for.

"I did the exposure," she said, "but the thoughts are still there. And I feel just as anxious."

"That's a great start," I told her. "But let me ask you . . . what did you actually *do* while you were in the kitchen?"

She looked confused. "I just . . . tried to tolerate being there. I held it for maybe thirty seconds, then put it away as quickly as possible. When the thoughts came, I reminded myself I'm a good mom who would never hurt anyone."

This was the perfect teaching moment about one of the most crucial distinctions in OCD treatment: There's a massive difference between being exposed and doing an exposure.

"What you're describing is being exposed," I explained. "You put yourself in an uncomfortable situation and white-knuckled your way through it until you could escape. You held the knife, which is great, but you mentally reviewed evidence that you're a good person."

Sarah nodded, recognizing the pattern.

"Doing an exposure is different," I continued. "It's purposeful and deliberate. It would mean not only holding the knife but actively leaning into the uncertainty. You'd hold it for longer periods of time. You might even smile as those intrusive thoughts start coming through. You'd be aware of any compulsions you may be doing at the time and resist the urge to do them.

"That sounds terrifying," Sarah admitted.

"It is at first," I agreed. "But here's the most important difference—how you respond to the thoughts when they come. Instead of mentally reviewing why you'd never hurt anyone or reminding yourself it's 'just OCD,' you'd respond with something like, 'Maybe I am dangerous. I'm willing to risk it,' or even 'I hope I do lose control. That would be interesting!' "

Sarah's eyes widened. "And I'd say this while holding a knife?"

"Yep! It's not about the knife. It's about the value your OCD is putting on it."

The Magic of "Maybe, Maybe Not"

When OCD throws a scary thought your way, your instinct is probably to fight it. To prove it wrong. To seek reassurance that it's not true. But what if you just left it uncertain?

The most powerful phrase in OCD treatment is surprisingly simple: "Maybe, maybe not."

OCD: "What if you get sick from touching that doorknob?"

You: "Maybe I will, maybe I won't."

OCD: "What if you actually hurt someone you love?"

You: "Maybe I will, maybe I won't."

OCD: "What if you chose the wrong career/partner/house?"

You: "Maybe I did, maybe I didn't."

This response is pure magic because it:

1. Accepts uncertainty (which is what OCD can't stand)

2. Doesn't engage in debate (which OCD always wins)

3. Is brief and almost boring (which gives OCD nothing to work with)

4. Can be applied to literally *any* obsession

"But isn't that dangerous?" Sarah asks. "To just say 'maybe' to these horrible thoughts?"

I smile. "Remember, we're not saying the thoughts are true. We're saying we can't have a hundred percent certainty about most things in life, and we're learning to be okay with that."

It's like when a toddler keeps asking why to everything you say, and after the fifteenth why, you finally say, "That's just how it is." You're not engaging with the endless questions anymore. That's what "Maybe, maybe not" does to OCD.

The first few times you try this, it's going to feel really weird. Like wearing someone else's shoes on your hands while trying to eat soup. Your brain is so used to jumping through elaborate hoops to answer OCD's questions that simply saying "maybe" feels almost rebellious.

But that's exactly the point. You're breaking a pattern.

You might practice saying "Maybe, maybe not" in the mirror. Get comfortable with the words. Say it with different tones—bored, mildly curious, slightly amused. Find what works for you. I'm a big fan of the "I don't care" attitude.

Just don't say it all panicked like you're in a horror movie: "MAYBE I WILL HURT SOMEONE . . . MAYBE I WON'T!" We're going for casual indifference here.

You might pretend you're a too-cool-for-school teenager when responding to OCD: "Whatever, OCD. Maybe that'll happen. Maybe not. I literally can't even with you right now."

You just did the voice, didn't you? You know the one I'm talking about. That slightly nasal, eye-rolling, gum-chewing voice where every statement sounds like a question? Where you mentally add "uhh" to the end of every sentence and imagine yourself twirling your hair while OCD desperately tries to get your attention?

That voice is *perfect* for responding to OCD. It captures exactly the right level of bored disinterest.

So go ahead and channel your inner sarcastic teenager. Roll those mental eyes. Let your responses drip with that "Why are you even talking to me right now?" energy. OCD has been the overbearing parent in your relationship for far too long. Time to flip the script.

The goal isn't to believe nothing bad will happen. It's to accept that certainty is impossible and to be okay with that. It's about becoming comfortable with "Maybe" as an answer, rather than demanding "Definitely not!"

Learning to Agree with the Threat

While "Maybe, maybe not" is a great starting point, you can take this line of thought even further by agreeing with the threat.

I can sense your inner terror as you read that. "*Agree with* my worst fear? Are you *crazy*, Nate?" But stay with me here, because this technique is so powerful, it can stop OCD dead in its tracks.

Instead of saying "Maybe, maybe not," try saying something like:

"Yeah, I hope I get sick from that doorknob. How fun would that be?"

"I definitely chose the wrong partner. I'm so excited about ruining my life."

"It would be great if I lost control right now."

Now, I know what you're thinking: "This sounds insane. Won't it make my thoughts come true?"

That's part of the whole process. We want words to be words. Thoughts to be thoughts. They don't have to mean anything unless we give them meaning. When you fight OCD, you give it power. When you agree with it, even in this exaggerated, almost sarcastic way, you take its power away.

Let me share a personal story that changed everything for me. Back in middle school, I had this bully who tormented me every day between classes. He would scream my name—"Peterson!"—and I'd feel that shock of dread as he came down the hallway. Every day it was the same: "You're so ugly," "Your nose is big," and on and on.

Day after day, I'd defend myself. "No, I'm not!" "I like my nose!" But he loved it. He fed on my desperation to prove him wrong.

Then one day, everything changed. He yelled, "Peterson!" and came charging down the hall as usual. "Your ears are big!" he taunted.

But this time, instead of defending myself, I tried something different. "Yeah, man, my ears *are* big! You're totally right! Actually, this one has, like, two bumps on it and this one has one bump. Thank you! I love it! My ears are *so* big right now. That's so cool!"

You should have seen his face. He was completely thrown. "What? Huh?" He had no idea what to say. And then he just . . . moved on. No joke—that was the last time he ever bullied me.

That moment changed my life because I realized agreeing with something takes all its power away.

To be clear: You don't actually believe these thoughts. You're not trying to convince yourself they're true. You're using a technique to short-circuit OCD's power.

But Sarah is understandably skeptical. "So when I have the thought that I might stab my kids, I'm supposed to say, 'Yeah, I probably will'? That feels . . . wrong."

She's right, in a sense. When it comes to certain themes like harm OCD, we should be more careful about how we apply this technique. But it still works. Rather than agreeing with the specific harmful action, I encourage her to focus on the core fear underneath it. For harm OCD, the core fear is often about losing control or being a bad person.

"So instead of saying, 'Yeah, I'll probably stab my kids,' you might say something like 'I hope I lose control someday. Really cool.' "

Sarah nods, looking slightly relieved. "That makes more sense."

Let's See These Responses in Action

If you're focusing too much on the specific content, you're missing the point. It's not about harm, religion, contamination, or whatever else. It's about the false signal OCD is sending, so agreeing disrupts it by throwing a ridiculous statement right back.

Here's what this might look like in practice:

CONTAMINATION FEARS

- "I hope this doorknob gives me the plague."
- "Maybe I'll get sick, maybe not. Either way, I'm not washing."

HARM THOUGHTS

- "Maybe I am a dangerous person. Maybe I'm not."
- "I hope I do lose control. That would make today interesting."

RELATIONSHIP DOUBTS

- "I might be with the wrong person. How exciting!"
- "Maybe I don't love them enough. I'll never know for sure."

RELIGIOUS WORRIES

- "God is mad at me. Pretty neat."
- "I hope that *was* a sin. I'm collecting them like trading cards."

"JUST RIGHT" FEELINGS

- "This feels wrong, and I'm not fixing it. How fun!"
- "Maybe it will bother me forever. I hope it sticks around."

SENSORIMOTOR OCD

- "I hope I notice my breathing forever. It's my favorite thing!"
- "It'd be great if my heart rate skyrocketed right now. I love this feeling."

Notice the light, almost playful tone in some of these. That's intentional. When you can respond to OCD with a touch of humor, you're sending a powerful message: *These thoughts don't define me, and they don't deserve my fear.*

How Your Body Can Talk Back to OCD

Here's something fascinating that most OCD books don't talk about: Your physical posture and movements can be as powerful as your verbal responses.

Think about it. When you're anxious, how does your body respond? You might:

- Hunch your shoulders
- Cross your arms protectively
- Fidget or pace
- Breathe shallowly
- Tense your muscles

All these physical responses tell your brain, "We're in danger! Act accordingly!"

But what if your body language said, "I'm not sure if I'm totally safe, but I'm willing to risk it and practice staying relaxed"?

When OCD triggers anxiety, you can try deliberately adopting relaxed body language:

- Lean back in your chair.
- Put your feet up.
- Let your shoulders drop.
- Place your hands behind your head.
- Smile or even laugh.
- Take slow, deep breaths.
- Move slowly.

This isn't about faking it till you make it. It's about using your body to send direct signals to your brain that contradict OCD's message of danger.

Sarah tries this in our session. As we discuss her knife fears, I ask her to lean back, put her feet up on another chair, and place her hands behind her head in the universal "I'm chilling" posture.

"This feels so wrong," she admits. "Talking about harming my kids while looking relaxed."

"Exactly," I tell her. "That contradiction is what makes it work. You're giving your brain conflicting information—the scary thought *and* the relaxed body. The body signals often win."

Research backs this up. The way we position our bodies directly impacts our emotional state and thought patterns. It's a two-way street: Our thoughts affect our posture, but our posture also affects our thoughts.

Try this right now: While you continue reading, deliberately adopt an exaggerated relaxed position.

Notice how much harder it is to feel panicked while physically signaling safety to your brain.

Finding the Right Tone: Not Too Much, Not Too Little

The way you say your response matters as much as what you say. If you say, "Maybe, maybe not," in a terrified whisper, it won't have the same effect as saying it with a casual shrug.

The ideal tone is:

- Casual and matter-of-fact
- Neither fearful nor aggressively confident
- Slightly bored, as if this thought isn't even interesting enough to get worked up about

A dash of sarcasm can be particularly effective. Remember that too-cool-for-school teenager voice? That slightly eye-rolling, "whatever" tone carries just the right amount of dismissiveness. It's like your OCD is that overdramatic friend who's always creating emergencies out of nothing, and you're the friend who's heard it all before.

"Oh no, I might get sick from this doorknob and die? Wow, that's totally original. Never heard that one before. Maybe I will, maybe I won't."

The sarcasm isn't directed at yourself, it's directed at the absurdity of OCD's constant catastrophizing. It's saying, "Come on, we both know you've predicted five hundred disasters that never happened."

Finding this tone can take practice, especially when your heart is racing from an OCD trigger. That's why it helps to rehearse your responses ahead of time, before the anxiety hits.

I often ask patients to record themselves saying their responses in this casual or slightly sarcastic tone, then play back the recordings during exposures. It's a great reminder of how to respond when you're in the moment.

Another helpful tip: Practice your responses while doing something mundane, like folding laundry or washing dishes. This helps your brain associate these statements with everyday normalcy rather than emergency situations.

Why These Responses Actually Work

You might be wondering why these response techniques work so well. Let me break down the science in simple terms:

Breaking the pattern: Your brain is used to a specific routine:

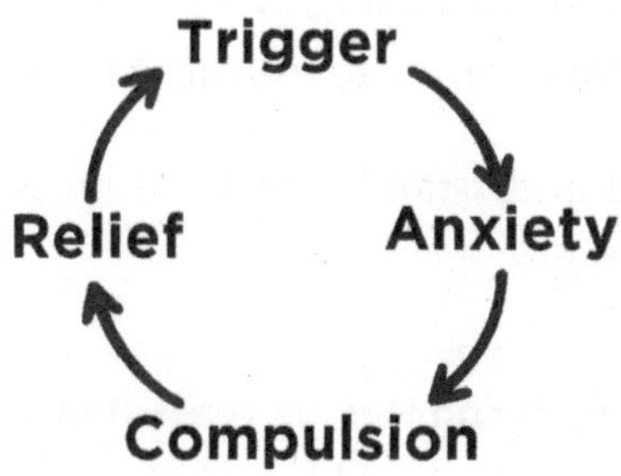

When you respond differently, you disrupt this pattern. It's like changing the route you take home. The old path gets less familiar over time.

Getting used to uncertainty: When you face your fears without doing compulsions, your brain gradually learns that uncertainty isn't actually dangerous. It's like swimming in cold water, which is uncomfortable only until your body adapts.

Processing emotions: These responses let you experience anxiety without trying to escape it. This helps your brain learn that anxiety will naturally decrease on its own, like a wave that rises and then falls.

Changing your beliefs: Over time, you start to think differently about uncertainty. Instead of seeing it as threatening, you begin to accept it as a normal part of life.

Think of it like creating a new path through a field. Each time you respond with "maybe" or agreement, you're walking that new path, making it more defined. Meanwhile, the old OCD path starts to grow over with weeds from lack of use.

Common Response Mistakes (and How to Avoid Them)

Even when you understand these techniques, it's easy to fall into common traps:

Mistake 1: Using responses as reassurance. Some people repeat "Maybe, maybe not" like a magic spell, hoping it will make anxiety go away. This turns the response itself into a compulsion.

Solution: Say your response once or twice at most, then move on. If you catch yourself thinking, "I have to say this or my anxiety won't go away," it might be turning into a compulsion.

Mistake 2: Self-reassurance. It's tempting to add reassurance: "I hope I get sick, but I don't really mean it" or "I'm a good parent and would never hurt anyone, but for OCD, I'm saying this phrase."

Solution: Remember that the content doesn't matter. We're just using words. Yes, somewhere in there, you know you're just acting. But we're not going to tell OCD this.

Mistake 3: The "just right" response trap. OCD may try to make you say your response in a certain way or a certain number of times until it feels "right."

Solution: Be deliberate about varying your responses slightly. Don't let them become ritualized.

Mistake 4: Waiting for anxiety to decrease. Some people use these techniques but still expect immediate anxiety reduction. When that doesn't happen, they think it's not working.

Solution: The goal isn't anxiety reduction in the moment. It's learning to function with anxiety present. Relief will come with practice over time.

When to Use Which Response

You have several response options now, but when should you use each one?

USE "MAYBE, MAYBE NOT" WHEN:

- You're just starting out with response techniques
- You want to practice uncertainty in all aspects of life
- You need a simple, universal response that works for any obsession

USE AGREEMENT WITH THE THREAT WHEN:

- You've been practicing for a while and are ready for something stronger
- You want to really take power away from obsessions
- You want some variety in your treatment

USE RELAXED BODY LANGUAGE WHEN:

- You notice your body tensing up during exposures
- You want to enhance the effect of your verbal responses
- You're in a situation in which speaking aloud isn't practical

Most people find that combining all three approaches works best. You might start with "Maybe, maybe not" while adopting a relaxed posture, then graduate to agreeing with the threat as you get more comfortable.

Real-World Examples

Let me share two real examples of how these responses work in everyday situations:

Example 1: Sexual Orientation OCD at a Party

Jordan has sexual orientation OCD and experiences intrusive thoughts about his sexuality when he's around attractive people of the same sex. He usually avoids social situations or leaves early when these thoughts hit.

His new approach:

- He goes to a party and stays near an attractive same-sex friend (exposure).
- When the thought comes—"What if I'm attracted to him? What if I'm gay?"—he responds with "Maybe I am, maybe I'm not."
- He deliberately relaxes his body.
- He prevents compulsions: no mentally reviewing past relationships, no avoiding eye contact, no leaving the party early, no asking his girlfriend for reassurance later.
- While sitting with anxiety he responds with a slight smile, "I hope I got my sexuality wrong. That would make things interesting!"
- When his brain says, "But what if you really are gay?" he responds with, "Well, then I guess I'd be gay."

The result: After he'd been doing this consistently for two weeks, the thoughts still came, but they no longer triggered the same level of panic. After a month, he could go the entire duration of social events without feeling the need to do compulsions.

Example 2: Contamination at a Restaurant

Elena has contamination OCD and avoids eating out because of fears about food poisoning. Previously, she would inspect every piece of food and ask servers detailed questions about food preparation.

Her approach:

- She goes to a restaurant and orders a salad (exposure).
- When the thought comes—"What if this lettuce has *E. coli*?"—she responds with "Maybe it does, maybe it doesn't. I'll find out!"
- She deliberately reclines in her chair, places her hands on the table, and takes slow bites while saying, "Let's go, *E. coli*, get in my belly!"
- When anxiety spikes, she escalates to, "I hope this salad *does* make me sick. I've always wanted to experience food poisoning!"

The result: The first few times were extremely difficult. But by the fifth restaurant visit, she was able to eat without needing to inspect her food or question servers. The occasional thought still popped up, but she found herself naturally responding with a mental shrug rather than panic.

Creating Your Personal Response Plan

Now it's time to create a personalized response plan using the obsessions you've already identified. Remember that tracking exercise from chapter 6? Time to put that information to work.

[Scan QR code.] →

For each of your main obsessions, write out:

- A "Maybe, maybe not" response that embraces uncertainty
- An agreement response that leans into the uncertainty
- A slightly sarcastic or humorous response that takes power away from the thought

Also describe the specific body language and physical adjustments you'll make when these thoughts arise.

Here's how Sarah filled it out:

OCD thought: "What if I lose control and stab my children with a kitchen knife?"

VERBAL RESPONSES:

- "Maybe I will lose control, maybe I won't."
- "I might be capable of doing something completely out of character. That would be interesting to discover."

- "Oh look, there's that thought again! *Yawn* . . . How original."

PHYSICAL RESPONSES:

- Leaning back against the counter; relaxed posture
- Slight smile or neutral expression

Working directly with your tracked obsessions makes this exercise much more powerful—you're creating responses for the exact thoughts that cause you the most distress.

The Process Takes Time

I need to be completely honest with you about something: These response techniques won't bring immediate relief at first. In fact, they might temporarily increase your anxiety.

That's normal and expected.

Remember, the goal isn't to make anxiety go away through these responses. The goal is to change your relationship with anxiety so it no longer controls your actions.

"How long before these responses start to feel natural?" Sarah asks.

"Everyone's timeline is different," I tell her. "But most people find that after two to three weeks of consistent practice, the responses start to feel less forced. After four to six weeks, they might even become your automatic reaction."

If you find yourself getting caught up in timelines, then your answer is, "I guess we'll see. I hope I *never* get used to using these phrases."

The key is consistent practice. These techniques aren't a one-and-done solution. They're skills that improve with repetition.

Think of it like learning a new language. At first, you have to deliberately think about each word and translate in your head. It feels awkward and unnatural. But with practice, the new language gradually becomes more automatic, until one day you realize you're thinking in that language without translating.

That's what happens with these response techniques. They become your new mental language.

Putting It All Together: Exposure + Response

The response techniques in this chapter aren't just tricks or hacks. They're fundamental shifts in how you relate to uncertainty, anxiety, and the contents of your mind.

But there's a crucial piece we still need to cover: the Prevention part of Response Prevention.

Think of it this way: We've learned how to create powerful exposures (chapter 7), and we've learned new ways to respond to intrusive thoughts in this chapter. But if we're still doing compulsions, it's like trying to drive a car with one foot on the gas and one foot on the brake.

That's why the next chapter is so important. We'll focus exclusively on how to prevent compulsions, both the obvious ones and the sneaky mental ones that keep you stuck. Without this critical piece, your new responses won't have the chance to create lasting change.

As you move forward with your OCD recovery, remember this: OCD has only as much power as you give it through your response. Change your response and you change the game.

"Maybe, maybe not. Either way, I'm okay with not knowing for sure."

That one response, practiced consistently and paired with prevention of compulsions, can change everything.

Chapter 9

Stopping Those Compulsions

You can create perfect exposures. You can craft brilliant "Maybe, maybe not" responses. But if you're still doing compulsions, you're trying to fill a bucket that has a giant hole in the bottom.

If we're being honest, the treatment could really be called "ER-P" because the Prevention part is so important it deserves to be separated out. But that sounds like we're heading to the emergency room, which sends entirely the wrong message. So ERP it is.

What *Is* Response Prevention, Anyway?

Response prevention is exactly what it sounds like: preventing yourself from doing the compulsive responses that keep OCD alive and kicking. It's about breaking the cycle where it matters most.

Think of it this way: If OCD is a fire, compulsions are the gasoline you keep pouring on it. Response prevention is finally putting down the gas can.

Here's what you're preventing:

- Physical compulsions (washing, checking, arranging)
- Mental compulsions (reviewing, counting, "figuring it out")
- Avoidance behaviors (skipping activities that trigger OCD)
- Reassurance-seeking (asking others if you're okay)
- Safety behaviors (subtle things you do to feel "safer")

All of these serve the same purpose: to reduce anxiety and gain certainty. And they all keep OCD thriving, like a well-fed pet that's learned exactly which tricks will earn it the most treats.

Why Prevention Is the Hardest Part

Response prevention is *hard*. Like, really hard. It's where my patients tend to struggle the most. Why? Because it requires doing something your brain is literally screaming at you not to do.

Picture this: Your anxiety is through the roof, every cell in your body is demanding relief, and the compulsion is right there, promising sweet, sweet comfort. It would be so easy to just . . . do it. Just this once.

Sound familiar?

That's why effective response prevention requires a fundamental shift in how you think about anxiety and uncertainty.

You need to move from:

"This anxiety is dangerous and I need to fix it *right now.*"

to:

"This anxiety stinks, but it's not dangerous, and it'll pass on its own if I let it."

This is much easier said than done. Your brain has been programmed to believe compulsions are necessary for survival. Breaking that programming takes time and practice. And a lot of courage.

The Rubber Band Effect

I like to think of OCD compulsions like a giant rubber band wrapped around your body, connecting you to your compulsion, making you feel trapped.

When you try to walk away from a compulsion, the rubber band stretches. The tension increases, growing stronger the farther you get from the compulsive behavior. As you keep moving away and resisting the compulsion, that rubber band stretches tighter and tighter. The tension becomes uncomfortable, even painful. Your brain screams, "Go back! Do the compulsion! Release the tension!"

And if you give in? *Snap!* The rubber band yanks you

right back to square one. The tension releases, and for a moment, you feel relief.

But here's what happens when you stay strong and keep moving: Eventually, if you stretch that rubber band far enough, it *breaks*.

And that's freedom.

This is why partial response prevention doesn't work. If you're 95 percent committed to not doing a compulsion but leave that 5 percent opening of "maybe just this once," you'll almost always get snapped back. The rubber band needs to break completely.

Building Your Response Prevention Game Plan

Response prevention sounds simple in theory—just stop doing compulsions, right? But in practice, it's more like trying to quit a habit that your brain has convinced you is keeping you alive. You need a clear plan.

Let's build that plan together.

[Scan QR code.] →

Step 1: Create your compulsion hit list

Remember back in chapter 6 when I asked you to track your compulsions? Time to dig up that sheet. If you skipped that step (I see you there, trying to sneak by), take some time right now to make a comprehensive list of all your compulsions.

And I mean *all* of them. The obvious ones, the sneaky

ones, and especially the ones you've been telling yourself "don't really count."

THE OBVIOUS, PHYSICAL STUFF

- Washing hands, showering, or cleaning like you're prepping for surgery
- Checking locks, appliances, or switches until your finger hurts
- Arranging things until they feel "just right" (whatever that means)
- Tapping, touching, or repeating movements a specific number of times
- Confessing thoughts or behaviors that are bothering you

THE SNEAKY, MENTAL STUFF

- Mentally replaying conversations like you're reviewing security footage
- "Canceling out" bad thoughts with good ones
- Counting in your head or repeating phrases silently
- Praying in specific patterns to neutralize thoughts
- Checking your heartbeat, breathing, or other body functions obsessively

- Analyzing feelings to determine if they're "right" or "normal"

THE AVOIDANCE GAME

- Not using certain words, numbers, or colors
- Taking weird routes to avoid "dangerous" places
- Not touching specific objects (knives, chemicals, etc.)
- Avoiding certain people or situations that trigger obsessions
- Procrastinating on decisions to avoid "making the wrong choice"
- Making other people do things you're afraid to do

THE REASSURANCE-SEEKING CIRCUS

- Asking others if you're okay or if you did something wrong
- Googling symptoms or fears like you're cramming for a medical exam
- Seeking second opinions (and third, and fourth . . .)
- Taking photos or videos of things you've checked
- Calling people to make sure they arrived safely

THE "SAFETY" BEHAVIORS

- Using paper towels to open doors
- Standing away from triggering objects
- Wearing certain "safe" clothes
- Adding extra steps to normal routines "just to be extra sure"
- Doing things in a specific order or with specific rules

Take a moment to really examine your list. Many people are shocked to discover they've been doing compulsions they never recognized as such. And if I didn't mention your specific compulsion, that doesn't mean you're unique and different and can't get better. It just means OCD is creative and I can't list every possible variation.

Step 2: Rate each compulsion

Once you have your list, rate each compulsion from 0 to 10 based on how difficult it would be to stop doing it. A 0 means it would be very easy to stop, while a 10 means it feels impossible right now.

Be honest here. No one is grading this.

Step 3: Start with a moderate challenge

Many people make the mistake of trying to eliminate their hardest compulsions first. This is like trying to run a marathon when you've never even jogged around the block. Instead, I recommend picking a compulsion in the 4 to 6 range: challenging enough to be meaningful, but not so hard you'll want to give up and binge-watch Netflix instead.

But here's the thing: You *can* start with what you think is the hardest if you want to. Treatment is flexible. Just because I suggest something doesn't mean it's the only way. You know yourself better than I know you. While it's natural to gravitate toward the easier exposures first, I'd encourage you to challenge yourself. Many people get comfortable staying with the easy stuff and then wonder why they're not seeing progress. Sometimes jumping into the deep end accelerates your growth in ways that tiptoeing around the shallow end never will.

Step 4: Create a specific prevention plan

For your chosen compulsion, create a detailed plan for exactly how you'll prevent it. Vague intentions like "I'll try to wash my hands less" are about as useful as a chocolate teapot.

Instead, get specific:

- How will I handle urges to do the compulsion?
- How can I make it more inconvenient to do the compulsion?
- What obstacles might come up?
- Who can support me in this process?

The more specific your plan, the better.

Step 5: One at a time (or not)

Some people focus on completely eliminating one compulsion before tackling another. They find more success in totally stopping one behavior than in partially working on five different ones.

Others prefer to work on multiple compulsions simultaneously. Both approaches work. Pick what feels right for you, not what you think you "should" do.

Sarah's Response Prevention Adventure

Sarah sits across from me in our latest session, looking noticeably more confident than when we started. Progress is progress.

"So," I begin, "what compulsion do you want to tackle first?"

She thinks for a moment. "Well, the handwashing is probably the biggest one, but that feels too scary to start with."

"Makes sense," I say, nodding. "What feels more manageable?"

"I've been asking my husband every night if he thinks I'm a good mom," she admits, looking slightly embarrassed. "Ever since those knife thoughts started, I need his reassurance constantly."

"That's a good one to target," I tell her. "How would you rate the difficulty of stopping that, on a scale of zero to ten?"

"Maybe a five?" she replies. "It would be really hard, but not impossible."

This is a perfect one to start with. Together, we craft Sarah's prevention strategy:

How will I handle urges to seek reassurance? *"When I feel the urge to ask, I'll notice the physical sensation of wanting to ask, take three deep breaths, and use my uncertainty statements like 'Maybe, maybe not.' Then I'll deliberately keep the conversation going about something else, knowing this is hard for me."*

How can I make it more inconvenient? *"I'm going to give my husband specific phrases to say if I ask for reassurance, like 'Maybe,' or 'Who knows?' So even if I slip up, I won't get the reassurance I'm looking for."*

What obstacles might come up? *"OCD will probably try to make me ask sneaky questions like 'Do I seem stressed with the kids?' or 'Do you think I'm being too hard on myself?' I need to recognize these are just backdoor reassurance-seeking. And I need to train my husband to spot them too."*

Who can support me? *"I'll explain the plan to my husband tonight. He needs to know I'm not stopping these questions because I don't value his opinion, but because I'm working on my OCD. I'll ask him not to offer reassurance even if I look upset."*

Strategies When Prevention Gets Really Tough

Even with the best plans, preventing compulsions can feel overwhelming. Here are some specific strategies for when the urge feels impossible to resist.

1. Delay the Compulsion

If not doing a compulsion feels completely impossible, start by delaying it. Tell yourself, "I'll wait five minutes before doing this compulsion."

During those five minutes, use your response statements:

- "Maybe something bad will happen, maybe it won't."
- "I hope something bad does happen. That would be interesting!"

After five minutes, reevaluate. Can you delay another five minutes? Often, delaying leads to the urge naturally decreasing, making it easier to skip the compulsion entirely.

2. Make Compulsions Inconvenient

Making compulsions harder to perform creates a pause between urge and action that helps break automatic patterns.

Some ideas:

- Keep only one soap, in an inconvenient location.
- Turn down the water heater temperature slightly (lukewarm handwashing is less satisfying).
- Put your phone in another room if you use it for checking.
- Remove browser bookmarks that make research easier.
- Mix your "safe" and "contaminated" clothes together.

The goal isn't to live this way forever, it's to insert awareness between urge and action, helping your brain reassess whether temporary relief is worth the extra effort.

3. Get Absorbed in Something Else

Choose an activity that requires your full attention, something that is engaging enough to compete with OCD's demands. This isn't distraction (which is just avoidance); it's strategic redirection.

Good options:

- Physical exercise
- Conversations with friends
- Creative activities
- Tasks requiring focus and problem-solving

These activities make it harder for your brain to simultaneously perform mental compulsions.

4. Use a Physical Reminder

Sometimes a physical reminder can strengthen your commitment. All you do is wear a rubber band on your wrist and snap it every time you have an intrusive thought . . . Just kidding; don't do that—it would be a compulsion! (I wish I could see your face right now.) The rubber band could be a visual reminder of your commitment. Others keep a small stone in their pocket to touch when urges arise.

5. Track Your Wins

Each time you successfully prevent a compulsion, record it. These small victories add up, creating evidence that you *can* resist compulsions.

A simple tally on your phone or check marks in a journal work well. Review these wins regularly to boost motivation when things get tough.

Don't Aim for Perfect

Here's something important that many OCD resources don't mention: You don't need perfect response prevention to get better.

You have permission to be human.

If you slip up and do a compulsion, that's what happened. That's life. You can feel better and live the life you want even if you hold on to a few compulsions along the way. If I had my way, I'd prefer you didn't give in to any of them—you don't need them—but give yourself some grace when you occasionally fall into a compulsion trap.

It's easy to get stuck in all-or-nothing thinking. "I missed the gym today and messed up this week. I'll start again next week." Sound familiar? It doesn't make sense, yet we do it all the time.

Common Obstacles and How to Handle Them

Let's address some common roadblocks and how to navigate them:

"I don't know if what I'm doing is actually a compulsion."

Sometimes the line between normal behavior and compulsions gets blurry. Ask yourself:

- Am I doing this to reduce anxiety?
- Would I do this if I weren't afraid?
- Does it feel necessary rather than chosen?

If you answered yes to any of these, it's likely a compulsion. And here's a secret: If you're even asking whether something is a compulsion, it probably is.

"I tried prevention, but my anxiety got worse."

This is expected! Anxiety often increases initially when you stop doing compulsions. This is the rubber band stretching. Keep going—remember, it needs to stretch before it breaks.

"I'm afraid something bad will happen if I don't do my compulsion."

This fear is the heart of OCD. Your brain has developed a powerful but incorrect belief that your compulsions are keeping you safe.

Think about how this association formed:

1. You had an intrusive thought that caused anxiety.
2. You did a compulsion to relieve that anxiety.

3. The anxiety temporarily decreased.

4. Your brain incorrectly learned: "That behavior prevented disaster."

It's like a baseball player who wore green socks during one winning game and now believes those socks are responsible for all future success. Your brain created a cause-and-effect relationship where none exists.

Logical explanations alone won't break this association. Your brain needs direct contradictory experience. When you prevent a compulsion and nothing bad happens, you're providing powerful evidence that contradicts the faulty belief system.

We can't be 100 percent certain something bad won't happen. We have to take the risk because living under OCD's rules isn't really living at all.

"I prevent obvious compulsions but find myself doing sneaky ones instead."

OCD is adaptable! When you block one compulsion, it often suggests alternatives.

You might switch from handwashing to using excessive sanitizer, or from asking "Am I a good person?" to making statements like "I feel so guilty" to fish for reassurance.

You might avoid asking direct questions but start telling "stories" about people with similar problems to gauge reactions.

Or you quit confessing specific thoughts but start sharing

detailed accounts of your day, hoping others will tell you everything was normal.

The key is recognizing that any behavior designed to reduce anxiety or gain certainty is likely a compulsion, even if it looks different from your original ones. OCD doesn't care what form the compulsion takes, it just wants you to keep feeding the cycle. When you catch yourself doing these sneaky alternatives, treat them exactly the same way you'd treat your obvious compulsions: Resist them and sit with the uncertainty instead.

"I feel guilty when I don't do certain compulsions."

This is particularly intense with moral or religious themes. OCD often targets your deepest values, creating a false equation: compulsion = morality.

Think about it: Did you need these exact rituals before OCD? Do other "good" people with the same values need to do them? Why are the rules different for you?

Someone with religious OCD might pray the same words over and over until it "feels right." But that's not what their faith actually requires.

Stopping compulsions isn't about giving up on being good. It's about breaking free from OCD's fake version of goodness so you can live by your real values again.

Response Prevention in Real Life

Response prevention happens in the messy context of real life. Here's how it might look:

AT WORK

- Trigger: Sent email to boss
- Compulsion to prevent: Reviewing sent emails repeatedly for typos
- Prevention strategy: Send email once, don't reread it, continue with other work tasks
- Response statement: "Maybe there's a typo, maybe not. I'm willing to risk it."

IN RELATIONSHIPS

- Trigger: Partner seems quiet
- Compulsion to prevent: Asking "Are you mad at me?" repeatedly
- Prevention strategy: Notice the urge, choose different conversation topic
- Response statement: "Maybe they're upset, maybe not. I can handle the uncertainty."

AT HOME

- Trigger: Going to bed
- Compulsion to prevent: Checking locks or stove multiple times
- Prevention strategy: Check once or not at all, then commit to staying in bed

- Response statement: "Maybe the house will burn down, maybe it won't. I'm willing to find out in the morning . . . if I'm still alive."

The key is making a conscious choice *not* to do the compulsion, even when anxiety is screaming at you.

How to Tell If It's Working

How do you know if your prevention efforts are paying off? Look for these signs:

SHORT-TERM WINS

- You resist compulsions more often.
- Anxiety decreases faster after exposures.
- You catch yourself before doing compulsions.
- You notice compulsions you weren't aware of before.

LONG-TERM PROGRESS

- Overall anxiety is lower.
- OCD thoughts have less emotional punch.
- You spend less time on OCD behaviors.
- You're engaging more in things you actually care about.
- The same triggers don't bother you as much.

Progress isn't a straight line. You'll have good days and rough days. Focus on the overall trend, not any single day.

But don't focus *too* closely on whether treatment is working. It's easy for this to become an obsession itself, one we call "meta-OCD." This is essentially having OCD about your OCD treatment!

If you find yourself constantly asking, "Is it working?" or "Am I doing this right?" give OCD a simple answer: "Maybe, maybe not."

Putting It All Together: The Complete ERP Picture

Now that we've covered all three components, let's see how they work together:

Exposure: You deliberately face things that trigger your OCD fears. This could be touching "contaminated" objects, writing out scary thoughts, or creating uncomfortable sensations.

Response: You practice specific verbal responses like "Maybe, maybe not" or "I hope something bad happens!" These responses embrace uncertainty rather than fighting it.

Prevention: You resist the urge to do compulsions, even when anxiety is high. This breaks the cycle that keeps OCD alive.

Together, they create a powerful method for retraining your brain and taking your life back from OCD.

I've Been Waiting for This Moment

I told myself that if I ever wrote a book, it would be free of boring stuff. People don't typically buy these books to learn about OCD—they buy them to find relief, guidance, and freedom.

I get so excited to give you all the answers that I want to skip all the previous chapters and just jump straight to building your complete treatment plan. Because creating a solid, personalized approach is what's going to help you get better. Thanks for sticking with me this far.

But guess what. We made it. We're here. We're doing this. Like, right now.

In the next chapter, we'll explore how to create a comprehensive ERP hierarchy and design a complete treatment plan that builds on everything we've covered.

You've got this. One prevented compulsion at a time, you're breaking those rubber bands and building a life of freedom.

Chapter 10

Creating an Exposure Hierarchy

Nine chapters in and you're probably thinking, "Enough already! When do I get to actually *do* something about my OCD?"

I hear you. We've covered the OCD cycle, learned about compulsions, talked about response techniques, and discussed how all themes work the same way. You've been patient with all the educational stuff, and honestly, you deserve a medal for making it this far.

But all that foundation work wasn't just me showing off. It's like learning to drive. You can't just hop in a car and hit the highway without understanding what the pedals do, right?

This is where theory meets practice. Where we turn all that understanding into actual change. We're about to create your personalized exposure hierarchy.

What Is an Exposure Hierarchy?

An exposure hierarchy is basically a list of things that trigger your OCD, organized from "mildly annoying" to "absolutely terrifying." As in a video game, you don't fight the final boss on level one.

The beauty of a hierarchy is that it breaks down the seemingly impossible task of "beating" OCD into bite-size pieces. Instead of trying to climb Mount Everest on day one, you're starting with hills, then mountains, then gradually working your way up.

Here's an example from responsibility OCD so you can see how hierarchies work across different types of OCD:

1. Reading about an ethical dilemma without solving it (2/10 anxiety)
2. Making a small mistake and not apologizing immediately (3/10 anxiety)
3. Telling a harmless white lie (4/10 anxiety)
4. Sending emails without triple-checking for mistakes (5/10 anxiety)
5. Writing "I hope they think I'm a bad person" and reading it aloud (6/10 anxiety)
6. Driving without checking rearview mirror excessively (7/10 anxiety)

7. Writing a detailed story about being selfish and cruel (8/10 anxiety)

8. Deliberately cutting someone off in conversation (9/10 anxiety)

9. Going around the house and turning the lamps on, risking a fire (10/10 anxiety)

Mining Your Tracking for Hierarchy Gold

Remember all that OCD tracking you've been doing? Those worksheets where you wrote down triggers, obsessions, anxiety levels, and compulsions?

Plot twist: That wasn't busywork! Those worksheets are pure gold for building your hierarchy.

This is where your detective work pays off. Your tracking should reveal:

1. **Specific situations** that trigger your OCD (doorknobs, knives, certain thoughts)

2. **How anxious** each trigger makes you (on that 0–10 scale)

3. **What compulsions** you usually do in response

If you haven't been tracking consistently (hey, no judgment), spend a few days really paying attention to what sets off your OCD before building your hierarchy.

Building Your Hierarchy: From "Meh" to "Absolutely Not"

Alright, let's actually build this thing. Here's the step-by-step process.

[Scan QR code.] →

Step 1: List your triggers

Write down all the situations, thoughts, objects, or sensations that make your OCD alarm bells go off. Be super specific. Don't just write "contamination." Rather, write "touching the shopping cart handle" or "using the bathroom at Target."

If you have harm OCD, instead of just writing "knives," get detailed:

- "Seeing a knife in the kitchen drawer"
- "Being near my kids while holding a knife"
- "Having a vivid thought about stabbing someone"

The more specific you are, the better your exposures will work.

Step 2: Rate each trigger

Now look at each trigger and estimate how much anxiety you think it would cause if you faced it without doing any compulsions. Use a 0 to 10 scale:

- 0–3: "I could probably handle this."
- 4–6: "This would be uncomfortable but doable."

- 7–8: "This would be really hard."
- 9–10: "This would be absolutely terrifying."

Here's the important part: You're just making educated guesses. You haven't actually done these exposures yet, so you're predicting. Your predictions might be totally wrong, and that's completely fine!

Don't get too caught up in the exact numbers. But if you're rating everything a 10, try comparing triggers to each other: "Would touching a public doorknob be more or less scary than touching a hospital doorknob?"

Also, do you know how many times I've heard someone say, "I don't think this will cause any anxiety," and when we test it out they say, "Ah . . . I was wrong"? You may have to test a few different actions even if you don't think they'd make you anxious.

Step 3: Organize from easiest to hardest

Line up your triggers from lowest anxiety rating to highest. This becomes the backbone of your hierarchy.

Remember, this isn't set in stone. You might discover that something you rated as a 5 actually feels like a 7 when you try it. Your hierarchy is a living document that you'll adjust as you learn more about your reactions.

Step 4: Fill in the gaps

Look for big jumps in your ratings. If you have something rated 4 and the next thing is 7, try to think of something that would fall around 5 or 6. If touching a doorknob at home is a 4 and touching a public bathroom doorknob is a

7, then touching a doorknob at a friend's house might be a 5 or 6.

Don't stress about getting these gap-fillers exactly right. The goal is just smaller, more manageable jumps between levels. If you're not sure what would fit, make your best guess.

Step 5: Add creative variations

For each level, think of different ways to practice the same exposure. If "using public bathrooms" is on your list, maybe include different types of restrooms like gas stations, restaurants, schools, or malls.

This is where you can get creative and maybe even have some fun with it. (Yes, I said fun. We're allowed to not be miserable 100 percent of the time.)

Maybe you practice the same exposure at different times of day, in various locations, or while your mood is different. The variations don't need to be dramatically different because small changes help your learning stick better.

Here's what Sarah's final hierarchy looked like:

SARAH'S EXPOSURE HIERARCHY

1. Looking at pictures of kitchen knives (2/10)

2. Watching cooking shows in which people use knives (2/10)

3. Being in the kitchen while my husband cooks with knives (3/10)

4. Holding a butter knife with my kids around (4/10)

5. Holding a chef's knife while alone (5/10)

6. Cutting vegetables with a chef's knife while alone (6/10)

7. Being in the same room as my kids with a knife visible (7/10)

8. Writing a story about losing control with a knife (8/10)

9. Preparing food with a knife while kids are in the kitchen (10/10)

Notice how Sarah's hierarchy focuses specifically on her harm OCD with knives. We could easily create a separate hierarchy for her contamination fears as well. Many people work with multiple hierarchies simultaneously, and there's no limit to how many items you can include on each one.

"This looks really challenging," Sarah admits, staring at her completed list.

"It is challenging," I agree. "But remember, you won't be doing the level ten exposure tomorrow."

The Full Exposure Package: It's More Than Just Actions

Here's something crucial: An effective hierarchy isn't just a list of scary situations. Each item needs several components to make it a complete exposure package.

Remember when we created Sarah's full exposure in chapter 7? We included four key pieces that make any exposure complete. Now let's apply that same approach to your hierarchy:

1. **The specific action** you'll take (what we've already listed)
2. **The verbal and physical responses** you'll use—your uncertainty phrases or threat-agreeing statements
3. **The compulsions you'll resist** doing (both obvious and sneaky ones)
4. **When and how often** you'll practice this exposure

Without these components, you might technically do the action but still engage in subtle compulsions that keep OCD alive. Or you might do it once but never repeat it enough for your brain to learn.

Make sure your response statements target your core fear directly. If your biggest fear is being a dangerous person, say something like "Maybe I am dangerous and have been fooling myself" rather than just "Maybe something bad will happen."

Making Your Plan Actually Doable

Creating a hierarchy is one thing, but sticking with it is another. Here are some practical strategies to make your ERP plan sustainable:

1. **Start with wins in mind.** Choose initial exposures where you're confident you can resist compulsions. Early success builds momentum for when things get tougher.

2. **Schedule exposures like real appointments.** Put them in your calendar with specific times. Treat them as nonnegotiable, just like a doctor's appointment or meeting.

3. **Build in accountability.** Tell someone about your plan. Find an "exposure buddy" who will check in on your progress, whether that's a therapist, relative, friend, or online support group member. "My husband can help keep me accountable," Sarah suggests. "He can check if I've done my exposures and remind me not to ask for reassurance."

4. **Track your progress.** Create a simple tracking system. This doesn't need to be fancy—a basic

notebook works perfectly. (Or use the worksheet—scan QR code.) For each exposure session, track:

- **Which exposure you did** (be specific: "Held butcher knife in kitchen")
- **Your anxiety before, during, and after** (using 0–10 scale)
- **Any compulsions you caught yourself doing** (be honest, no judgment)
- **How long you stayed with the exposure**
- **Notes for next time** (What did you learn? How can you improve?)

"I didn't think tracking would matter much," Sarah tells me, "but looking back at my early entries has been eye-opening. Three weeks ago, holding a butcher knife was a five out of ten anxiety. Now it's barely a one."

Seeing progress on paper can be incredibly motivating when things get tough. On rough days when it feels like nothing's changing, your tracking provides concrete evidence of how far you've come.

5. **Plan for setbacks.** They will happen, so have a strategy ready:

- If you have a particularly bad day, commit to doing at least one small exposure.
- If you give in to compulsions, write down what happened without judgment, then try again.
- If an exposure feels too hard, scale it back slightly rather than avoiding it completely.

6. **Connect to your values.** Remind yourself why you're doing this difficult work. Go back to your motivation work from chapter 6.

And here's something important: Keep living your life! If you want to go bowling but you're afraid of contamination, go bowling anyway. If you want to exercise but you're nervous about your heart rate, exercise anyway. Live life on your terms, not OCD's.

But . . . How Do I Do an Exposure for My Theme?

Despite knowing that we treat all themes the same, many still wonder how to do an exposure for their theme. While each person's core fear may be different, here are examples of what an exposure could look like for each theme of OCD. Don't just skip to your OCD theme, because there is benefit in seeing the pattern we use for different exposures. It may spark some ideas for your own exposure hierarchy.

CHECKING OCD

- **Action:** I'll leave my home without checking locks, stove, or other appliances more than once.
- **Verbal/physical response:** As I walk out the door, I'll say, "Maybe I left something dangerous on. I hope my house burns down!" while deliberately walking with a relaxed, unhurried pace.
- **Compulsions to resist:** I won't return to check, won't ask someone else to check, and won't mentally review when I last used each appliance.
- **When:** I'll do this every time I leave home and at random intervals throughout the day.

CONTAMINATION OCD

- **Action:** I will set at least twenty timers on my phone that remind me to stand up, run around my house, and touch as many things as I can for thirty seconds. I will then continue doing whatever I was doing without washing my hands.
- **Verbal/physical response:** I'll take any threat and agree with it. "I hope I get sick, that'd be fun" or "I'm loving this gross feeling right now."
- **Compulsions to resist:** I won't use sanitizer or wash my hands.
- **When:** Random intervals throughout the day when my timer goes off.

DISGUST OCD

- **Action:** I will walk around my house and touch things my brain says would make me feel gross, like the trash. If it's really bothering me, I'll make sure to rub my hands on my clothes to spread it around.
- **Verbal/physical response:** As I touch it, I'll say, "Yes, this is totally disgusting and I love it. I hope I feel this all day."
- **Compulsions to resist:** I won't wash my hands immediately, won't change clothes, won't use sanitizer, won't avoid touching my phone or doorknobs after.
- **When:** I'll do this three times daily.

EMOTIONAL CONTAMINATION OCD

- **Action:** I will deliberately spend time with someone I fear has "negative energy" or bad luck that might transfer to me.
- **Verbal/physical response:** "I sure hope I lose all my luck today and start making negative choices. That'd be pretty neat."
- **Compulsions to resist:** I won't avoid the person, wash after contact, throw away items they touched, engage in mental rituals to "cleanse" myself of their influence.

- **When:** I will do this at least three times a day, and if they aren't around, I'll look at a picture of them.

EXISTENTIAL OCD

- **Action:** I'll watch videos of people speaking about the possibility that life has no inherent meaning.
- **Verbal/physical response:** While watching, I'll write down, "Maybe, possibly, sure" to any threat that my brain produces, as I lean back in my chair with relaxed shoulders.
- **Compulsions to resist:** I won't seek comfort in spiritual texts and won't mentally ruminate to "solve" the question.
- **When:** I'll do this twice before work and three times after work.

FALSE MEMORY OCD

- **Action:** I'll write out the thought "I may have done something terrible that I've forgotten" and read it aloud several times daily.
- **Verbal/physical response:** As I read it, I'll shrug and say, "Maybe I did, maybe I didn't," without tensing my muscles or changing my breathing.
- **Compulsions to resist:** I won't review evidence, won't ask others what they remember, and won't try to get "clarity" about the memory.

- **When:** I'll do this four times daily, especially when feeling anxious about past memories.

HARM OCD

- **Action:** I will spend fifteen minutes drawing pictures of things that trigger me, like knives, bridges, and guns.
- **Verbal/physical response:** While drawing, I'll say, "Maybe these images reflect my true desires, maybe they don't," as I continue with steady hand movements and a relaxed posture.
- **Compulsions to resist:** I won't tear up the drawings, won't add speech bubbles saying, "I'd never do this," won't seek reassurance about what the drawings mean.
- **When:** I'll do this four times a day, during my work breaks.

HEALTH ANXIETY

- **Action:** I'll read about serious diseases online for fifteen minutes while noting any physical sensations I experience.
- **Verbal/physical response:** "Maybe reading about this disease means I actually have it."
- **Compulsions to resist:** No checking my body for

the symptoms I just read about, no seeking reassurance, no researching to "rule out" conditions.

- **When:** I'll do this twice daily, morning and evening.

"JUST RIGHT" OCD

- **Action:** I'll set timers to go off throughout the day. When they do, I will walk around touching, looking at, and engaging with things until I feel the need to redo something.
- **Verbal/physical response:** I'll say to myself, "Oh man, I love this feeling inside. I hope it lasts all day," as I smile with confidence and walk away.
- **Compulsions to resist:** I won't do anything to fix the feeling. I won't retouch, count, or mentally try to get the "just right" feeling.
- **When:** I'll do this multiple times daily when the timer goes off.

MEMORY HOARDING OCD

- **Action:** I'll delete five photos from my phone each day without reviewing them first.
- **Verbal/physical response:** As I delete them, I'll say, "I might regret losing these memories, I might not," without hesitating on the delete button.

- **Compulsions to resist:** I won't back them up first, won't screenshot them, won't try to memorize details before deleting.
- **When:** I'll do this every morning and evening, gradually increasing the number of photos.

PEDOPHILIA OCD (POCD)

- **Action:** I'll volunteer to babysit or spend time with family members' children while being present with any anxious thoughts that arise.
- **Verbal/physical response:** When anxiety spikes, I'll say, "Maybe these thoughts mean something about me, maybe they don't," as I maintain relaxed body language and continue normal interactions.
- **Compulsions to resist:** I won't mentally review interactions for "inappropriate" feelings, won't seek reassurance, and won't avoid normal childcare activities.
- **When:** I'll do this three to five times weekly in planned situations.

PERINATAL/POSTPARTUM OCD

- **Action:** I'll bathe my baby alone without asking my partner to supervise.
- **Verbal/physical response:** While bathing them, I'll

take any perceived threat in my mind and answer it with an uncertainty statement: "Maybe, maybe not" or "Eh, cool thought."

- **Compulsions to resist:** I won't call someone to watch me, won't avoid holding my baby over the water, and won't repeatedly check that they're okay.
- **When:** I'll do this during regular bath times.

PURELY OBSESSIONAL (PURE O) OCD

- **Action:** I'll set at least fifteen timers to go off throughout the day. When they do, I will write down all the thoughts I have for two minutes.
- **Verbal/physical response:** "Cool thought bro. Thanks for these. You're welcome to stick around."
- **Compulsions to resist:** I won't counter it with "good" thoughts, won't analyze why I had it, and won't seek mental certainty about what it means.
- **When:** I'll do this daily, randomizing the times my timers go off.

REAL EVENT OCD

- **Action:** I will write a detailed story of the past event as if it's happening right now. I will add details of what I see, hear, and feel. I will read this over and over again.

- **Verbal/physical response:** I will take any threat that comes to my mind and leave it uncertain or agree with it. I will read the story without judgment.
- **Compulsions to resist:** I won't confess repeatedly, won't seek reassurance about moral character, won't mentally review the event, and won't check for evidence of harm caused.
- **When:** I will read this story at least ten times a day.

RELATIONSHIP OCD

- **Action:** I'll write for fifteen minutes, completing the sentence "What if I don't really love my partner because . . ." with as many reasons as I can think of.
- **Verbal/physical response:** After writing, I'll say, "Maybe I've been lying to myself this whole time. I hope I picked the wrong person and will be miserable! That would be fun," as I lean back in my chair with a casual, slightly amused expression.
- **Compulsions to resist:** I won't balance with positive statements, won't seek reassurance from friends, and won't review "evidence" of my love.
- **When:** I'll do this at least three times a day when my alarm goes off on my phone.

RELIGIOUS SCRUPULOSITY

- **Action:** I'll say my prayers while making deliberate small mistakes or allowing "bad" thoughts to be present.
- **Verbal/physical response:** After finishing, I'll say, "I might have just invalidated my entire prayer. Maybe God is disappointed in me now!" as I continue with my normal activities.
- **Compulsions to resist:** I won't start over, won't apologize to God, and won't say extra prayers to "make up for it."
- **When:** I'll do this daily during my regular prayer time.

SEXUAL ORIENTATION OCD

- **Action:** I'll watch movies/shows with attractive people of the gender that causes doubt, while noticing any reactions without judgment.
- **Verbal/physical response:** When noticing reactions, I'll say, "Maybe this means something about my sexuality. Maybe it doesn't. I'm okay with not knowing for sure!" as I recline comfortably on my couch.
- **Compulsions to resist:** I won't analyze my reactions, won't check for arousal, and won't compare how I feel about different genders.

- **When:** I'll do this three or four times weekly, during my regular evening TV/movie time.

SOMATIC/SENSORIMOTOR OCD

- **Action:** I'll focus intently on my breathing for fifteen minutes without trying to control it.
- **Verbal/physical response:** As I focus, I'll think, "Maybe my breathing is wrong, maybe it's not," while sitting still without adjusting my posture.
- **Compulsions to resist:** I won't distract myself from the sensation, won't try to breathe "correctly," and won't check if others are breathing the same way.
- **When:** I'll do this twenty-five times a day, especially in quiet moments when awareness naturally increases.

SUICIDAL OCD

- **Action:** I'll walk across bridges while allowing thoughts about jumping to exist in my mind.
- **Verbal/physical response:** When the thoughts come, I'll say, "Maybe I'll jump, maybe I won't," as I continue walking at a normal pace and with a smile.
- **Compulsions to resist:** I won't avoid looking down, won't rush across the bridge, and won't repeatedly reassure myself that I don't want to die.

- **When:** I will cross one new bridge or overpass daily and walk back and forth at least five times.

If you just made it through all of these, good job! I hope you were able to gain some clarity about how exposures work. As you may have noticed, everyone's goals are different. While some focus on once a day, others may do twenty-five or more. Your job is to focus on what makes sense to you, while continuing to push yourself.

Order vs. Randomization: Two Approaches to Hierarchy

There are actually two approaches to tackling your hierarchy:

The gradual approach: This is what we've discussed so far, starting with easier items and gradually working up as anxiety decreases. This approach is:

- More structured
- Often less overwhelming
- Confidence-building
- Effective for most people, especially beginners

The random approach: Some therapists advocate using dice or cards to determine which exposure to do next, regardless of difficulty level.

"Wait, why would anyone want to randomize it?" Sarah looks confused.

"Good question," I respond. "The theory is that when

you randomize exposures, your brain doesn't categorize some fears as worse than others. All uncertainty becomes equal, which can speed up learning."

The random approach can:

- Be more challenging but potentially more efficient
- Help break the hierarchy mindset (the idea that some fears are "bigger")
- Prevent avoidance of harder exposures
- Work well for people with some ERP experience

"I've had clients literally roll dice to decide which exposure to do next," I tell Sarah. "Or use a deck of cards with different exposures written on each one."

"That sounds terrifying," Sarah admits.

"It can be," I acknowledge. "But some people find it liberating to remove the decision-making process. There's no debating whether you're 'ready' for a harder exposure. You just do whatever comes up."

I generally recommend starting with the gradual approach and maybe incorporating randomization as you gain experience. Both work; the most important thing is consistency.

As Sarah leaves my office, hierarchy in hand, she pauses at the door. "So once I start doing these exposures, how will I know when it's time to move up?"

I smile. "That's exactly what we'll talk about next time."

In the next chapter, we'll tackle the questions that inevitably come up once you've begun doing exposures:

- How do you know when it's time to move to the next level?
- What signals tell you treatment is actually working?
- How often should you be doing exposures to see progress?
- What kind of timeline can you realistically expect?

Your exposure hierarchy is ready. Your response prevention plan is clear. You understand your OCD's patterns better than ever. Now it's time to put this knowledge into action and start climbing that staircase—one step at a time.

Chapter 11

I Did an Exposure . . . Now What?

You've created your hierarchy. You've designed your exposures. You've even started facing some of your fears. And now you're wondering what's next.

This is where many people get stuck with two common problems:

1. They do the same exposure forever, never challenging themselves further (like that person at the gym who's been doing the same workout for three years).

2. They rush through exposures too quickly, never giving their brain time to learn.

Finding the right balance is key. So let's talk about exactly how to know when to move up your hierarchy and how to tell if all this uncomfortable work is actually making a difference.

When to Move up the Hierarchy

I often see clients get comfy with one level of exposure. It's not easy, but it feels manageable. And there's a strong temptation to just camp out there forever.

But effective ERP is about growth, not comfort. You need to keep challenging yourself to see real progress. (Sorry, your brain doesn't get to retire to Florida just yet.)

Here's how you know it's time to level up:

Your anxiety has dropped by at least half

If touching that doorknob used to spike your anxiety to an 8/10 and now it's hanging around a 3/10, that's your cue.

Notice I said "hanging around." Not just that one magical Tuesday when you felt great. I'm talking about doing the exposure multiple times and seeing that reduced anxiety stick around. (One good day doesn't make you recovered any more than one salad makes you healthy.)

But here's something important: Your anxiety might not drop much, and that's okay too.

The exposure feels boring

Sometimes your anxiety doesn't plummet, but the exposure starts feeling . . . well, boring. Like, "Oh great, touching doorknobs again. How thrilling."

This is actually fantastic! Your brain might still feel anxious about the uncertainty, but it's getting bored with the specific trigger. It's like saying, "Yeah, I'm still not sure if this doorknob is contaminated, and that uncertainty still makes me nervous, but honestly . . . I'm kind of tired of thinking about doorknobs."

When you first touched that doorknob, your entire focus was glued to it. But now you can touch it while half listening to a podcast or thinking about what to have for lunch. That's your brain getting bored with the uncertainty surrounding your specific exposure.

You can resist compulsions without much effort

If you can go through multiple sessions without running off to wash your hands, seek reassurance, or do whatever your particular OCD dance moves are, you've probably mastered that level.

Early on, you might catch yourself doing sneaky compulsions even while trying not to. (OCD is like a toddler and will find ways to get what it wants.) But over time, you get better at spotting and stopping them.

You're doing it naturally in real life

The goal isn't just to do exposures during special "exposure time." It's to naturally engage with triggers in your everyday life.

Like when you casually grab a knife to make lunch without having to give yourself a pep talk first. Or when you use a public bathroom without it being a whole production worthy of Broadway.

You've been consistent

One successful exposure doesn't mean your brain has learned everything. Your brain needs repetition to actually change its programming.

If you've been doing the same exposure regularly for a week or so and you're seeing the described signs, you're probably ready to move up.

A Word on "Feeling Ready"

"But what if I'm not actually ready?" Sarah asks. "What if I just think I am, but then the next level totally destroys me?"

Oh boy. See what just happened there? That's OCD trying to sneak back in and create doubt about your progress.

The question isn't "Am I ready?" It's "Am I *willing*?" Are you willing to try the next exposure even though it might be uncomfortable? Even though you might not handle it perfectly? That willingness is all you need. The idea of tolerating uncertainty lies in all aspects of your life, even the decision to go to the next step on your hierarchy.

What If You Feel Stuck?

"Okay, but what if I've been doing the same exposure for weeks and nothing's changing?" Sarah asks. "Like, it's not getting easier, but it's not getting worse either. I'm just . . . stuck."

This happens more than you'd think. Sometimes you hit a plateau, and it can be frustrating. Here are some strategies for those:

Check your response prevention game

Often when people feel stuck, they're not actually stuck. They're just missing some subtle compulsions. Are you really, truly resisting all your compulsions? Even the sneaky mental ones?

Get honest with yourself. Are you secretly reassuring yourself? Are you doing the exposure in a "safe" way that doesn't actually challenge you? Sometimes getting honest about your compulsions can help you break through.

Mix it up a little

If you've been holding a knife at home alone, try holding it with someone else in the room. Or in a different location. Or when you're tired versus when you're alert.

Small variations can sometimes kick-start learning again. Your brain might have gotten too comfortable with the exact scenario you've been practicing.

Refresh your response statements

Are your "Maybe, maybe not" statements starting to feel stale? Try switching them up. Maybe try agreeing with the thought instead: "Yeah, maybe I will get sick from this doorknob. I hope it happens. What an amazing experience that would be."

Sometimes a fresh approach can reengage your brain's learning process.

Get some outside perspective

Sometimes we're not the best judges of our own progress. A therapist, support group, or trusted friend who understands

ERP can offer perspective on whether you're truly stuck or just being impatient.

The Danger of Moving Too Fast

On the flip side, some people have the opposite problem: They try to sprint through their hierarchy like they're training for the Olympics.

"Maybe if I just force myself through all the hard exposures really fast, I can be done with this whole thing," they think.

ERP isn't about checking exposures off a list. It's about giving your brain time to learn new associations. Moving too quickly doesn't allow that learning to happen.

If you find yourself rushing, try to reconnect with why you're doing this work. This isn't about getting it over with—it's about creating lasting change in your brain. And that takes time.

How to Tell If Treatment Is Working

"How do I know if this is actually working? Sometimes I still have the thoughts. Sometimes I still feel anxious."

This is a question almost everyone asks at some point. And it's critical to be clear about what "working" actually means in ERP. Because many people have the wrong idea, and it sets them up for disappointment.

Misconception 1: Successful ERP means no more intrusive thoughts

This is simply not true, and it's one of the most damaging misconceptions about recovery. Everyone has intrusive thoughts, even people without OCD. Those thoughts about harm, contamination, or making mistakes? They pop into non-OCD brains too. The difference isn't the presence of the thoughts; it's the reaction to them.

I often tell clients to imagine two people who both have the thought, "What if I left the stove on?" The person without OCD thinks, "Huh, weird thought," and goes about their day. The person with OCD thinks, "Oh no, what if I did? What if the house burns down? I think I checked it, but what if I don't remember checking correctly?" The initial thought is identical. It's the response that differs.

The goal of ERP isn't to never have another intrusive thought again. That's not possible for the human brain. The goal is to *change your relationship* with those thoughts so they don't control your behavior or cause significant distress.

Successful recovery means a thought can pop in and you can acknowledge it without getting hooked by it. The thoughts may still come (maybe less frequently, maybe not), but they'll be more like background noise rather than blaring alarms.

Misconception 2: Successful ERP means no more anxiety

This misconception leads many people to give up too early. They do exposures but still feel anxious sometimes, and they think it's not working. Anxiety is a normal, necessary human emotion that everyone experiences. Even the most mentally healthy people feel anxious sometimes!

Anxiety itself isn't the problem. It's a normal bodily response designed to protect us. The problem is when anxiety becomes excessive and starts controlling what you do or don't do. When it shrinks your life.

You can say, "I still feel anxious when my triggers show up, but now I face them anyway and live my life." That's success! You might not be fully anxiety-free, but anxiety is no longer calling the shots.

Successful ERP doesn't eliminate anxiety; it builds your tolerance for it. It teaches your brain that you can feel anxious and still function. You learn that anxiety isn't dangerous, just uncomfortable, and you can handle uncomfortable feelings.

It's common to hear this and think, "So I'll feel anxious forever? What's the point of treatment?" I get why that feels hopeless. But you might be thinking about it the wrong way. Just like getting used to a recurring sound in your house, like the refrigerator humming or the heater clicking on, anxiety can become background noise. If it's there, it just exists. It only has power when you give it attention.

Misconception 3: Success means perfect exposures

OCD loves to whisper that unless you're doing exposures perfectly, they don't count or won't work. This is a trap. Perfectionism is incredibly common with OCD, and it often extends to the treatment itself.

I see this all the time: "I tried to resist checking, but I checked once, so I completely failed." Or "I had a thought during my exposure that wasn't part of the plan, so I must be doing it wrong."

The reality is that there are no perfect exposures. No OCD therapist expects perfection from their clients. What matters is consistency and effort, not flawless execution.

A "good enough" exposure that you actually *do* is infinitely more valuable than a "perfect" exposure that exists only in your mind. If you catch yourself doing a subtle compulsion mid-exposure, that's not failure—it's awareness! Notice it, get back on track, and keep going.

So What Does "Working" Actually Look Like?

Recovery isn't always obvious when you're in the middle of it, especially because progress often happens gradually. Here's what real treatment success actually looks like, broken down by timeline.

SHORT-TERM SIGNS

- You notice your response to triggers changing (still have the thought, but don't panic).
- You get better at catching compulsions (awareness is huge!).
- Your anxiety might be slightly less intense or doesn't last as long.
- You can do things you couldn't do before (even small things count).

- You recognize OCD's tricks faster ("Oh, there's that 'this is different' argument again").

LONGER-TERM PROGRESS

- You're doing activities OCD previously prevented.
- You spend less time on OCD behaviors overall.
- Intrusive thoughts cause less distress.
- You handle setbacks better.
- ERP skills become woven into daily life without thinking about it.

When You Don't Feel Different

"I've been doing exposures for two weeks," Sarah tells me. "Some days feel better, but other days it's just as hard as when I started. Is that normal?"

Absolutely. And this is where a lot of people get discouraged and quit.

When you don't feel noticeably different, it doesn't mean treatment isn't working. Here's why:

Change is gradual

Brain rewiring happens slowly. It's like watching a kid grow. If you see them every day, you might not notice the changes. But someone who hasn't seen them in months will say, "Wow, you've grown so much!" Recovery can be like that.

Others notice first

Family members or friends often spot improvements before you do:

- “You’re not asking for reassurance as much.”
- “You seem more present at dinner.”
- “You handled that uncertainty really well just now.”

If people are commenting on changes, pay attention. They might be seeing progress you can’t see yet.

Progress doesn’t always feel like progress

Sometimes getting better actually feels worse temporarily. When you become more aware of your compulsions, you suddenly start noticing behaviors you used to do on autopilot. This awareness, though uncomfortable, is actually huge progress.

Feelings come last

The behaviors change first, then the thoughts, and finally the feelings. So if you’re doing exposures consistently even though you still feel anxious, that’s progress! The feelings will catch up eventually.

The Bottom Line

As we wrap up, let’s circle back to the main question: “How do I know if treatment is working?”

The simplest answer is that treatment is working if you're doing things *differently* than before.

If you're facing fears instead of avoiding them, that's working. If you're letting thoughts be thoughts instead of emergencies, that's working. If you're practicing sitting with uncertainty instead of desperately seeking certainty, that's working.

The feelings might take time to catch up. The intrusive thoughts might still show up. Some days might still suck. But if you're responding differently to OCD, then yes, treatment is working.

In our next chapter, we'll tackle something crucial: staying consistent with your exposures. Because knowing what to do is one thing. Actually doing it consistently, especially when motivation tanks? That's where the real work happens.

Chapter 12

Sticking with the Plan

Sarah walks into my office with a spring in her step. It's been a month since we created her exposure hierarchy, and I can see the subtle changes in her demeanor. Her hands are less raw, she's making eye contact more consistently, and there's a hint of confidence in her voice that wasn't there before.

"I did it," she announces proudly as she sits down. "I used a knife to make dinner while my kids were in the kitchen. I even let my daughter help me chop veggies with a butter knife."

"That's fantastic," I tell her, genuinely excited by her progress. "How did it feel?"

"Scary at first," she admits. "But I kept reminding myself, 'Maybe I'll lose control, maybe I won't,' and just focused on cooking. By the time dinner was ready, I was barely thinking about it."

This is what progress looks like—not the absence of anxiety, but the ability to function despite it. Sarah is starting to reclaim parts of her life that OCD stole from her.

But then her smile falters slightly.

"But I've been meaning to ask you something," she continues, her voice more hesitant now. "How do I keep this going? Some days I'm motivated and can do hard exposures, but other days . . . I just don't want to face it. And there's this part of me that's terrified I'll slide back to where I was before."

Sarah has just identified one of the biggest challenges in OCD recovery: consistency. It's not enough to know what to do or even to do it occasionally. Real, lasting change requires sticking with your plan when motivation fades, life gets busy, or anxiety spikes.

In this chapter, we're going to tackle exactly that—how to create a sustainable treatment plan that you'll actually follow, how to track your progress, how to push through when excuses arise, and how to use your support system to keep going when things get tough.

Creating Your Exposure Calendar: The Power of Planning

If there's one thing I love, it's a calendar. You know why? Because for the most part, most people do not keep exposures at the top of their to-do list. Why would you? It means *choosing* to schedule time to feel anxious.

"How often should I be doing exposures?" This is one of the most common questions I hear. Is daily better than three times a week? Should you do them in the morning or evening? For fifteen minutes or an hour?

Let me clear this up right now: There's no single "perfect" schedule that works for everyone. But there are principles that can help you create an effective plan for your unique situation.

The most successful recovery plans share these characteristics:

1. **They're consistent and predictable.** Your brain learns through repetition. Doing exposures on a regular schedule helps your brain form new pathways more efficiently than sporadic, random practice.

2. **They're sustainable for *your* life.** A plan you can maintain for months is infinitely better than an "ideal" plan you abandon after a week.

3. **They include multiple types of exposures.** You want a mix, with some challenging ones, some easier maintenance ones, some quick ones, some longer ones.

4. **They're written down and visible.** They're not just floating around in your head, where OCD can easily talk you out of them.

So . . . How Much Is Enough?

This is a tricky question because the answer depends on several factors:

- The severity of your OCD
- How much time you realistically have available
- How many different OCD themes you're addressing
- Your current level of functioning

Here's my general guideline: Aim for **at least 30 to 60 minutes of dedicated exposure work daily**, plus incorporating exposure principles into your everyday life whenever possible.

That might look like:

- One thirty-minute planned challenging exposure
- Several five-minute, quick exposures throughout the day
- Applying response prevention all day long

Remember, ERP isn't just something you do during designated "exposure time." It's a way of responding to OCD whenever it shows up in your life.

Many see remarkable progress with just thirty minutes of dedicated practice daily, while others benefit from more intensive approaches. What matters most isn't the exact amount, but your consistency and commitment to the process.

If you were to go to an intensive outpatient program for OCD, you'd be expected to do exposures at least three hours a day, and that's just in the office. Then you'd go home and possibly do another three.

Those who do these programs can progress very quickly. What do you think they are doing differently than the average person? *Lots of exposures!* But of course, dedicating six hours a day to OCD exposures isn't realistic for most of us.

Creating Your Personalized Calendar

Now let's get practical. Take out your paper or digital calendar and let's block out your exposure time for the next two weeks.

1. **Choose consistent time slots.** When are you most likely to follow through? Some people like mornings, before the day gets hectic. Others prefer evenings, when they have fewer responsibilities. Some need to schedule exposures for lunch breaks or while commuting.

2. **Start with frequency, not duration.** It's better to do fifteen minutes daily than two hours once a week. Consistency trumps intensity, especially when you're building the habit.

3. **Be specific about which exposures you'll do.** Don't just write "Do exposure" on your calendar. Write "Read triggering articles without checking facts" or "Write out harm script and read it 3 times."

4. **Include preparation and processing time.** If you schedule a twenty-minute exposure, give yourself five minutes before to prepare mentally and five minutes after to record your experience.

5. **Build in accountability.** Will you text your support person when you complete the exposure? Will you track it on your phone? Will you review your progress weekly?

Here's what Sarah's calendar looks like for one week:

MONDAY

- 7:00 A.M.: Use kitchen knife to make breakfast (5 min.)
- 12:30 P.M.: Write script about losing control (15 min.)
- 3:00 P.M.: Read script over and over again while using response prevention (15 min.)
- 7:00 P.M.: Help kids with homework without checking for germs (30 min.)

TUESDAY

- 7:00 A.M.: Touch bathroom doorknobs without washing (5 min.)
- 1:00 P.M.: Walk around the house and touch things my brain says not to (5 min.)
- 5:30 P.M.: Cook dinner with sharp knife while kids are home (30 min.)
- 9:00 P.M.: Record progress in journal (10 min.)

WEDNESDAY

- 7:00 A.M.: Use kitchen knife to make breakfast (5 min.)
- 12:30 P.M.: Read harm script from Monday (15 min.)
- 4:00 P.M.: Go grocery shopping and touch 30 "contaminated" items (20 min.)
- 8:00 P.M.: Practice response statements while looking at triggering news stories (10 min.)

And so on for the rest of the week.

Notice that Sarah's plan includes:

- Short daily exposures (knife at breakfast)
- Longer, more challenging exposures (cooking with kids present)
- A mix of in vivo and imaginal exposures
- Regular time for tracking and reflection
- Both contamination and harm OCD exposures

When you create your own calendar, refer back to your hierarchy from chapter 10. Choose exposures that challenge you but don't completely overwhelm you. Remember, we're aiming for sustainable practice, not a single heroic effort followed by avoidance.

Tracking Your Progress: What Gets Measured Gets Improved

Remember that QR code worksheet I mentioned earlier about tracking your exposures? Now's the time to scan it if you haven't already.

[Scan QR code.] →

Tracking your exposures serves several crucial purposes:

1. **It creates accountability.** You're less likely to skip planned exposures when you know you'll have to record them.

2. **It provides objective evidence of progress.** On days when it feels like nothing is changing, your tracking sheet can show you how far you've come.

3. **It helps identify patterns.** Maybe you notice you consistently avoid exposures on busy workdays or that certain types of exposures are harder than others.

4. **It builds momentum and motivation.** Seeing a streak of completed exposures can motivate you to keep the streak alive.

I know I keep saying it, but this is the key insight: Progress isn't just about feeling less anxious; it's about reclaiming your life despite the anxiety.

The Excuse-Busting Tool Kit: When OCD Tries to Negotiate

Let's get real: There will be days when you don't feel like doing exposures. Days when OCD whispers (or shouts) all the reasons why today is not a good day to challenge yourself.

Here are the top excuses OCD will try to use, and how to bust through them:

Excuse 1: "I'm too tired/busy/stressed today."

This is OCD's favorite opening move. It sounds so reasonable! After all, self-care is important, right? But here's the truth: Doing your treatment *is* self-care. It's the most important thing you can do for your well-being.

Excuse-buster: "I don't need to feel energized to do an exposure. In fact, learning to face uncertainty even when I'm tired builds stronger skills."

Excuse 2: "I'll start tomorrow/next week/after this stressful period is over."

This is the perpetual postponement trap. There will always be a reason to put it off if you're looking for one.

Excuse-buster: "OCD doesn't wait for a convenient time to bother me, so I won't wait for a convenient time to fight back. I can do a shorter or easier exposure today, but I won't skip it entirely."

Excuse 3: "I'm doing well, so I don't need to do exposures today."

This is a particularly sneaky one. You're feeling good, which must mean you can take a break, right? But consistent practice is what got you feeling better in the first place.

Excuse-buster: "I'm doing well *because* of my consistent practice. Taking a break from exposures when OCD is quieter is like stopping antibiotics when you start feeling better, because it increases the chance of a relapse."

Excuse 4: "This feels too hard right now."

When anxiety is high, exposures can feel impossible. Your brain convinces you that you're not capable of handling the discomfort.

Excuse-buster: "I don't have to do the hardest exposure on my hierarchy. I can choose something manageable, but I will do something. Taking action, no matter how small, builds momentum."

Excuse 5: "I'm not sure if I'm doing this right."

The fear of doing exposures "incorrectly" can prevent you from doing them at all. Just do something. Even if you're unsure.

Excuse-buster: "Imperfect exposure practice is infinitely more effective than perfect avoidance. I'll do my best with what I know right now, and adjust as I learn more."

Sarah experienced this firsthand when she caught herself putting off knife exposures because she was "too tired" after work. We created a modified plan for those days—five minutes of just holding a knife while using her response statements.

"It's not as challenging as my full cooking exposure," she admitted, "but it keeps me in the habit of facing my fears instead of avoiding them."

Exactly. Sometimes success is simply refusing to let OCD win the day, even if your exposure is brief or simplified.

Handling Setbacks: When Things Don't Go as Planned

Let's talk about one of the most important skills in OCD recovery: handling setbacks. Because they will happen. I promise you that.

You might have a day (or week) when you:

- Skip planned exposures
- Do exposures but engage in subtle compulsions
- Face a spike in symptoms after a period of improvement
- Find yourself avoiding triggers again
- Seek reassurance or perform other compulsions

The difference between people who recover from OCD and those who stay stuck isn't whether they experience setbacks. It's how they respond to them.

The Setback Action Plan

Here's a simple three-step plan for handling setbacks:

Step 1: Notice without judgment

When you realize you've had a setback, simply notice it without harsh self-criticism. "I notice I've been avoiding kitchen knives again this week" is more helpful than "I'm such a failure, I'll never get better."

This nonjudgmental awareness is crucial because shame and self-criticism often lead to more avoidance, creating a negative spiral.

Practicing self-compassion during setbacks

Try this exercise when you catch yourself being self-critical.

[Scan QR code.] →

Recognize the critical voice. Write down the exact words your inner critic is saying. For example: "I'm so weak. I should be better at this by now. Everyone else would be making faster progress."

Imagine a friend. Now imagine a good friend was in your situation and told you they were thinking these thoughts. What would you say to them? Write down your response. It might be: "Recovery isn't linear. Having a hard week doesn't erase all your progress. Remember how far you've come from where you started."

Talk to yourself with that same compassion. Now rewrite your original self-critical statement using the compassionate tone you'd use with a friend. "I'm having a hard time right now, which is normal in recovery. This setback doesn't define me or erase my progress. I can take small steps to get back on track."

Physical self-compassion gesture. Place your hand on your heart or give yourself a gentle hug. This physical gesture can activate your body's soothing response system and reduces the stress chemicals that shame produces.

Remember, setbacks are not a reflection of your worth or strength. They're a normal part of any change process.

Step 2: Get curious about what happened

Ask yourself:

- What triggered this setback?
- What thoughts, feelings, or situations led to avoiding exposures or doing compulsions?
- What was different about this situation compared with times I've been successful?
- What do I need right now to get back on track?

This curiosity helps you learn from setbacks rather than being demoralized by them.

Challenge negative thoughts with evidence

When setbacks lead to negative thinking patterns, try this exercise:

1. **Identify the thought:** "This setback means I'll never recover from OCD."

2. **Identify the thought distortion:** This is "all-or-nothing" thinking and "fortune-telling" (predicting the future negatively without evidence).

3. **Gather evidence that contradicts the thought:**
   - "I've had setbacks before and still made progress afterward."
   - "I was able to do exposures successfully last month, which proves I'm capable."

4. **Create a balanced alternative thought:** "This setback is temporary and doesn't erase my previous progress. Recovery includes ups and downs, and I can learn from this experience."

Challenging a thought this way can be helpful when it deals with negative thoughts about yourself. However, be careful not to use this with specific OCD obsessions or intrusive thoughts, as it tends to provide self-reassurance.

Step 3: Take action, no matter how small

The most important step is to do something—anything—that gets you moving back in the right direction. This might be:

- Doing a small, manageable exposure
- Reviewing your tracking sheet to remind yourself of past successes

- Reaching out to your support person
- Reconnecting with your motivation and values

"RESTART" ACTIONS YOU CAN TAKE TODAY:

1. **The five-minute commitment:** Promise yourself you'll do just five minutes of exposure work. Set a timer. Often, once you start, you'll end up continuing beyond the five minutes. But even if you only do that, you've broken the avoidance pattern.

2. **The hierarchy reset:** If you've been avoiding exposures completely, go back two or three steps on your hierarchy to an easier exposure that feels manageable. Success with an easier exposure rebuilds confidence and momentum.

3. **The physical reset ritual:** Sometimes you need a physical way to "reset" after a setback. Try taking a shower, changing your clothes, going for a walk, or doing ten jumping jacks. As long as it's not a compulsion, any physical action that creates a sense of starting fresh will work.

4. **The visual reminder:** Look at a photo, object, or written statement that reminds you why you're fighting OCD. Keep this visible during your restart exposure.

5. **The accountability call:** Call or text your support person with a specific plan: "I'm going to touch the bathroom doorknob without washing my hands in the next hour, and I'll text you when I've done it." External accountability can provide the extra push needed after a setback.

Remember that action comes before motivation. You don't need to feel ready or confident to restart, you just need to take that first small step.

Sarah experienced a significant setback after a particularly stressful week at work. She found herself avoiding the kitchen again and asking her husband to cook instead. When she realized what was happening, she felt discouraged.

"I thought I was past this," she told me. "It felt like all my progress disappeared overnight."

We worked through the setback action plan together:

Notice: *"I've been avoiding cooking for about a week now."*

Get curious: *"It started after I had that big presentation at work. I was exhausted and stressed, and OCD took advantage of that vulnerable state. My brain convinced me I needed a 'break' from exposures."*

Take action: *Sarah decided to do a small kitchen exposure that evening, just holding a knife while standing in the kitchen for five minutes. She also added a note to her calendar to be extra vigilant about keeping up with exposures during stressful periods.*

The small exposure wasn't much, but it broke her avoidance pattern.

When Motivation Fades: Connecting to Your Values

Let's address one of the most common challenges in maintaining any long-term change: fading motivation.

In the beginning, you might feel highly motivated to beat OCD. You're in pain and your desire for relief is strong. But over time, as you start making progress and having better days, that initial motivation can wane.

This is why connecting your exposure practice to your deeper values is so important. Values-based motivation is more sustainable than pain-based motivation.

Remember your "rock" from chapter 6—that core motivator that keeps you going when things get tough? Now's the time to reconnect with it.

Ask yourself:

- What matters most to me that OCD interferes with?
- Who am I doing this hard work for?
- What kind of life do I want to be living one year from now?
- What would I be doing differently if OCD weren't running the show?

Sarah's rock was being present for her children. She wanted to be able to play with them, cook for them, and be the mother she wanted to be without OCD interfering.

"On days when I don't feel like doing exposures," she

tells me, "I look at a photo of my kids on my phone. It reminds me that I'm putting myself through this discomfort so that I can be fully present in their lives."

The Long Game: This Is a Marathon, Not a Sprint

As we end this chapter, I want to emphasize something important: OCD recovery is not a quick fix. It's not about doing perfect exposures for a few weeks and then being "cured" forever.

It's about creating a sustainable approach to uncertainty and anxiety that you can maintain over the long term.

"How long will I need to keep doing exposures?" Sarah asks during one of our sessions.

"There's no single answer to that," I tell her honestly. "But think of it like physical fitness. You might need intense, frequent workouts at first to build strength. Eventually, you'll reach a maintenance phase where you need less, but you'll still need some ongoing practice to maintain your gains."

Many people find they need intensive daily practice for several months to see significant improvement. After that, they might shift to a maintenance schedule with less frequent but still regular practice.

But here's what I've observed in my many years of treating OCD. My patients who make the most lasting progress are those who don't just do exposures, but integrate the principles of ERP into their entire approach to life. They learn to:

- Notice when OCD is starting
- Choose to face uncertainty rather than avoid it
- Respond to intrusive thoughts with acceptance rather than resistance
- Prioritize their values over temporary comfort

When you build these skills into your daily life, ERP becomes less something you *do* and more something you *live*. Which sets us up for the next chapter. Exposures aren't a one-and-done thing. They're a lifestyle, and I'm going to show you how to make them part of your life.

Chapter 13

Living a Lifestyle of Exposure and Aftercare

Sarah walks into my office looking . . . relaxed. That's the best way I can put it. Her hands aren't raw anymore. She's not fidgeting. She makes eye contact when we talk, instead of staring at the floor like her shoes hold the secrets to the universe.

"I've been doing really well," she tells me, and I can hear the surprise in her voice. "I cooked dinner for my family three times last week, with actual sharp knives and everything. I wash my hands, like, only when I need to. And those scary thoughts about hurting my kids? They still pop up sometimes, but instead of freaking out, I'm like, 'Oh hey, there's that weird thought again. Whatever.'"

I can't help but smile. "That's awesome, Sarah. You've done the hard work, and it shows."

She nods, then gets that look people get when they're about to ask *the Question*. "So . . . am I cured now? Like, is this where we high-five and I skip off into the sunset, never to be bothered by OCD again?"

Ah, there it is. The question I hear from pretty much everyone who's made good progress. It makes total sense—after weeks or months of doing scary stuff on purpose and resisting the urge to do compulsions, you'd hope there's a finish line where OCD just . . . goes away forever.

"Not exactly," I tell her, trying to be gentle. "Think of it more like learning to live with a really annoying roommate who you can't kick out, but you've finally figured out how to not let them boss you around."

Sarah's face falls a little. "So . . . I'll always have OCD?"

"You'll always have a brain that sometimes gets stuck in the OCD loop," I clarify. "But that doesn't mean you'll always struggle like you did before."

I grab a piece of paper and draw a squiggly line that goes up and down but generally trends upward. (My artistic skills are about as good as my ability to fold a fitted sheet, but it gets the point across.) This is recovery:

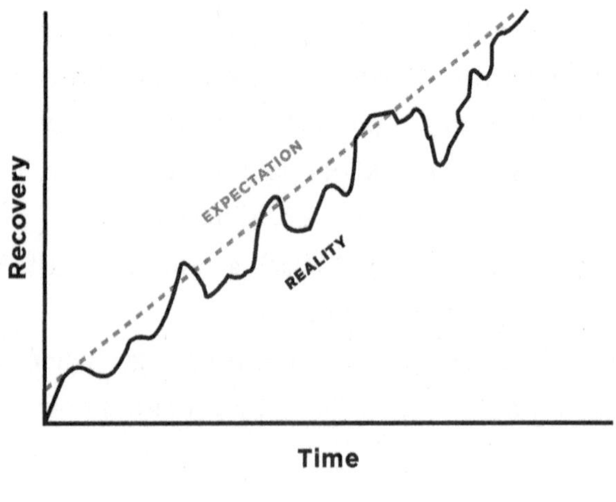

Sarah studies my wonderful drawing. "So . . . doing exposures forever?"

"Kind of, yeah," I reply, nodding. "But not the crazy intense stuff you've been doing. More like . . . remember when you first learned to drive? You had to think about every little thing, like checking mirrors, signaling, and braking gently. Now you probably drive to work half-asleep while mentally planning your grocery list. Same thing here—now it becomes second nature."

This is what I want you—yes, you reading this right now—to get. ERP isn't just something you do for a few months and then forget about. It's more like a new way of living.

In this chapter, we're going to talk about how to turn ERP from an intense boot camp into a chill lifestyle that keeps you free from OCD's nonsense without taking over your whole life. We'll cover practical ways to maintain your progress, and what maintenance actually looks like in real life.

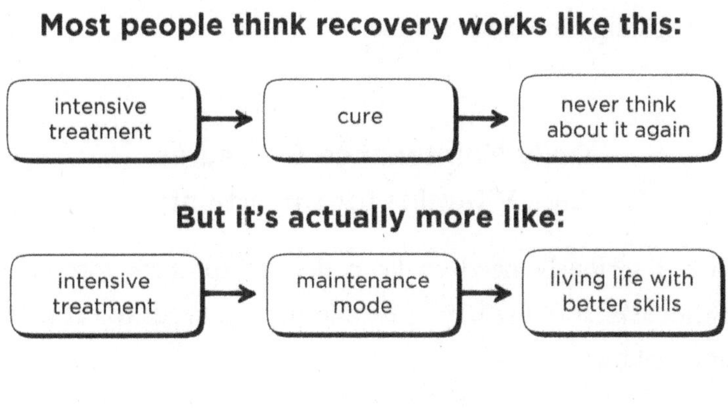

The Shift to Maintenance Mode

You've been doing exposures consistently, your anxiety is more manageable, and life feels more normal. So now what? This is where many people get confused about what recovery actually looks like.

OCD MAINTENANCE HAS A FEW PARTS:

1. **Quick daily "maintenance exposures":** Small daily habits that keep your uncertainty skills sharp.
2. **Living with uncertainty in everyday life:** Using your ERP principles in regular situations, not just OCD triggers.
3. **Staying alert for sneaky compulsions:** Watching out for behaviors that might be creeping back in.
4. **Having a plan for rough patches:** Because they happen, and it helps to know what to do.

Let's dig into each of these.

Daily Maintenance Exposures: Like Vitamins for Uncertainty

"Do I seriously need to keep doing exposures forever?" Sarah asks, looking like I just told her she needs to eat kale at every meal.

"Not the intense stuff," I reassure her. "But yeah, some small daily practice helps keep your skills sharp."

This isn't about making yourself anxious every day. It's about staying friends with uncertainty through tiny, regular reminders.

Pick one or two super simple, daily exposures that take just a few seconds but remind you how strong you are. For Sarah, this might be:

- Touching a kitchen knife for five seconds every morning while she makes breakfast
- Looking at a picture of a gross public bathroom that she keeps on her phone
- Writing the word *contaminated* with a big ol' smile once each day

The key is linking it to stuff you already do.

"So it's like . . . a tiny daily reminder that I can handle uncertainty?" Sarah asks.

"Exactly," I tell her. "When you do these quick exposures, remind yourself: 'This used to feel impossible, and now it's just a few seconds of my Tuesday.' "

The magic is in doing it every day. A sixty-second daily exposure is way more valuable than a thirty-minute exposure once a month. You're building uncertainty into your daily routine, making it feel normal instead of like a big, dramatic event.

"Every single day?" Sarah asks. "That actually sounds easier than trying to remember to do big exposures twice a week."

"Right?" I nod. "When something becomes part of your

daily routine like brushing your teeth or checking your phone multiple times before noon, you don't have to think about motivating yourself. It just becomes what you do. You also don't have to let go of the big exposures; they have value too."

For these daily exposures to work, they tend to:

- Be quick (under thirty seconds)
- Target your main fear directly
- Happen every day (or close to it)
- Feel more like a gentle reminder than a major challenge

Remember, these aren't about creating anxiety, they're about staying friends with uncertainty. If they start feeling completely automatic and boring, that's perfect!

Here are some examples for multiple themes:

- Focus on your heartbeat without checking if it's "normal" while brushing teeth.
- Write "Maybe I'll snap today. Cool" on a sticky note while eating breakfast.
- Send an email without proofreading it multiple times during your lunch break.
- Leave one thing on your desk slightly "not right" while leaving work.
- Look at a picture of your spouse while saying, "I'm glad I picked the wrong person."

- Hold scissors for ten seconds while waiting for the water to warm up.
- While scrolling social media, look at an attractive person without analyzing.
- Write "Maybe I have a serious illness" on paper before getting in the shower.
- While getting dressed, notice a body sensation without googling it.
- Write "Maybe nothing is real" on a piece of paper while eating lunch.
- Read about an ethical dilemma without solving it during your lunch break.
- Leave the house without checking locks/stove when heading to work.

You can create routines that you do every day. Use sticky notes with triggering words and put them up in your house. Give them high fives when you see them. Find ways to make maintenance easy. If you have to go out of your way to make it happen, it probably won't.

Life Is Uncertain: Deal with It

While specific exposures are important, the real magic happens when you start using ERP principles in regular life. And here's something cool to think about: You're already dealing with uncertainty all day long. You just might not realize it.

Think about it. When you wake up, you don't know if traffic will be bad, if your coworker will be in a good mood, or if it'll rain later. You don't know if your favorite restaurant will be crowded, if that text you're waiting for will come today, or if your computer will decide to have a meltdown.

Most people handle all this uncertainty without breaking a sweat. They just . . . live with it. They make decisions with incomplete information. They go about their day without needing to know everything in advance.

So here's the practice: Instead of trying to eliminate the uncertainty that's already there, start noticing it and purposely sitting with it. Better yet, create a little more of it on purpose.

MORNING UNCERTAINTY PRACTICE

- Don't check the weather before getting dressed. Just pick something and see what happens.
- Leave for work without checking traffic apps. Take whatever route you want.
- At the coffee shop, don't order your usual drink. Tell the barista to make you their favorite.

WORK UNCERTAINTY PRACTICE

- Share an idea in a meeting without rehearsing it first.

- Make decisions with 80 percent of the information instead of 100 percent.
- Delegate a task without micromanaging how it gets done.

SOCIAL UNCERTAINTY PRACTICE

- Text someone without crafting the perfect message.
- Make plans without knowing every detail in advance.
- Go to a party without knowing exactly who will be there or what you'll talk about.

EVENING UNCERTAINTY PRACTICE

- Watch a movie without reading reviews first.
- Try a new recipe without watching YouTube tutorials.
- Go to bed without checking your alarm for the third time.

The goal isn't to be reckless. It's to practice being comfortable with the "I don't know" that's already part of life. When you catch yourself trying to eliminate normal uncertainty, pause and ask, "What if I just . . . didn't know this thing? What if I was okay with that?"

Sarah laughs when I explain this. "I never thought about it that way. I spend so much energy trying to know things that . . . I probably don't actually need to know."

Sarah is exactly right. Most of life happens in the *maybe zone*, even if we like to trick ourselves otherwise.

Here's a fun challenge: Try to go one full day without googling anything. Don't look up that actor's name, don't check what time the store closes before leaving, don't verify that random fact your friend mentioned. Just . . . let the questions exist without answers.

When a real problem shows up, then solve it. Problem-solving is meant for actual issues you can see, not imaginary ones your brain invents.

This is uncertainty strength training. The more you practice being okay with not knowing small stuff, the easier it becomes to handle the bigger uncertainties that OCD throws at you.

Building Your Personal Aftercare Plan

Now let's get practical and create your personal aftercare plan, which is basically your road map for staying free from OCD's shenanigans long-term.

[Scan QR code.] →

Think of this like creating a personalized workout routine, except instead of building muscle, you're maintaining your freedom from OCD. The key is making it specific to you and the progress you've already made.

1. Your daily maintenance exposures

Start by looking back at your hierarchy. Which exposures have you mastered? What used to feel impossible that now feels manageable? Those are your gold mines for maintenance.

Pick one or two of these "conquered" exposures and turn them into tiny daily reminders of your strength. Ask yourself:

- Which exposure used to terrify me that I can now do easily?
- How can I do a mini-version of this every day?
- When during my existing routine can I fit this in?
- What do I want my brain to keep learning?

The goal isn't to make yourself anxious. It's to remind your brain: "Hey, remember when this used to be scary? Look how strong we are now."

Sarah picks two things she's conquered:

- Kitchen knives (she can now cook dinner with her family without freaking out)
- Public contamination (she can touch doorknobs without washing immediately)

So her daily maintenance becomes:

- Touch a knife for five seconds while making breakfast (she always makes eggs anyway).
- Hold her office doorknob for a few seconds when arriving at work without washing her hands afterward (she has to open it anyway).

"What do you want your brain to keep learning from these?" I ask her.

"That uncertainty is okay," she says. "That I can handle scary thoughts. That I don't need to know everything for sure."

2. Your uncertainty practices

This is where you take your ERP skills and apply them to regular life stuff. Think about areas where you still try to control or know everything:

- What do you still research to death before deciding?
- What do you still check multiple times?
- What small imperfections do you still fix immediately?
- What normal life uncertainties do you still try to eliminate?

Sarah's identified areas

- She googles symptoms when she feels a little off.
- She checks her phone repeatedly to make sure she didn't miss a message.
- She sets multiple alarms even though she always wakes up on time.

Her uncertainty practice plan

- Notice a physical sensation and say, "Maybe it means something; maybe it doesn't."

- Put her phone in another room and wait an hour before checking it.
- Set one alarm and trust it.

3. Your support system

Recovery maintenance works better when you're not doing it alone. Think about:

- Who understands your OCD journey?
- Who can gently call you out if you start slipping back into old habits?
- Who can you text when you're having a tough day?

Sarah identifies:

- Her husband (who learned to stop giving reassurance)
- Her OCD support group (monthly meetings)
- Her sister (who also struggled with anxiety)

Your Personal OCD Fire Drill

One of the most helpful tools I give people is what I call an "OCD Fire Drill"—a specific plan for what to do if you notice OCD gaining strength again.

[Scan QR code.] →

Just like families practice fire drills,

having a clear plan for OCD flare-ups gives you confidence and keeps small bumps from becoming major crashes.

Step 1: Know your early warning signs

What signals might mean OCD is flaring up? For Sarah:

- Taking longer than twenty seconds to wash her hands
- Asking her husband more questions about the kids
- Hesitating before using kitchen knives
- Avoiding triggers she used to handle fine

Step 2: Have an immediate action plan

What will you do when you notice these signs? Sarah's plan:

- Go back to daily doorknob exposures.
- Hold a knife for one minute while being present with all harm thoughts.
- Text her support group.
- Reschedule specific exposures to do throughout the day.

Step 3: Prepare kind self-talk

What will you tell yourself? Write these down now:

- "This is just a bump in the road, not a total failure."
- "I've gotten through rough patches before."

- "The fact that I notice this shows how much I've learned."

Step 4: Practice your fire drill

Mentally walk through your plan so it feels familiar when you need it.

This mental practice makes it way more likely you'll actually use your plan when OCD pressure increases.

The Weird Truth About Freedom

As we wrap up, Sarah looks at her aftercare plan. "It still feels like a lot," she admits. "Part of me hoped that once I did enough exposures, I could just be done with thinking about all this."

I nod. "I get it. But here's the weird thing about OCD recovery. Real freedom doesn't come from never having to deal with OCD again. It comes from knowing you can handle it when it shows up."

This might sound backward, but ongoing practice is what creates lasting freedom.

Think about learning to play guitar. At first, your fingers hurt, you have to think about every chord, and you sound like a dying cat. But with practice, your fingers find the right spots automatically. You don't stop playing guitar; you become a guitarist. The skills that once felt like torture become the source of your ability to play any song you want.

Same thing with OCD recovery. The practices that once felt like work gradually become your new normal. You don't stop practicing; you become a person who naturally handles uncertainty differently.

"So I'll always be 'in recovery?'" Sarah asks.

"In a way, yeah," I tell her. "But that doesn't mean you'll always be struggling. Most people who keep up their practice find that OCD takes up less and less space in their lives over time. The maintenance becomes as automatic as brushing your teeth."

Living an exposure lifestyle doesn't mean constantly fighting OCD. It means consistently choosing freedom over fear, choosing flexibility over rigidity, and living your values instead of avoiding discomfort.

Your Journey Keeps Going

As our session winds down, Sarah gathers her stuff and stands up with a new confidence I haven't seen before.

"So this isn't really the end," she says. "It's more like . . . graduating from OCD boot camp to real life."

"Exactly." I smile. "The skills you've developed aren't just for managing OCD. They're life skills that make you stronger in all kinds of ways."

This is my message to you too, reader. The work you've done isn't just about beating OCD—it's about developing a totally different relationship with uncertainty and discomfort. These skills will make you more adaptable when life throws curveballs. More present in your relationships. More willing to take healthy risks and grow.

As you keep going, remember:

- Small, consistent practice beats occasional heroic efforts.
- You already have all the skills you need; now it's just about using them consistently.
- Every time you choose to face uncertainty, you make yourself stronger.
- You're not alone in this journey.

Your maintenance plan isn't just about keeping OCD from coming back. It's about creating a life in which uncertainty becomes an okay, even interesting part of your experience instead of something terrifying.

And that, my friend, is real freedom.

You're not just recovering from OCD. You're becoming an uncertainty expert in a world that desperately needs people who can handle the unknown with courage and grace.

Chapter 14

Your Support Network

There's no way to sugarcoat this: Getting your family involved in your OCD treatment can be awkward and uncomfortable. But it's also one of the most powerful tools to make sure your recovery lasts.

Why Nobody Wants to Ask for Help (but You Should Anyway)

Let's start with the truth. Asking your family to help with your OCD treatment feels weird for about seventeen different reasons:

1. **You have to acknowledge your compulsions out loud.** "Hey honey, can you stop telling me I'm a good person when I ask? It's actually feeding my OCD." Awkward.

2. **You're asking them to watch you suffer without helping.** This goes against every instinct loving people have.

3. **You're essentially training them to be "mean" to you.** At least that's how it feels.

4. **You have to explain OCD to people who probably don't get it.** "So when I ask if I'm contaminated, just say maybe instead of no." (Cue the confused stares.)

5. **You're admitting you need help.** For many people, this feels like failure.

But after years of watching families navigate OCD treatment, let me tell you: The people who love you *want* to help. They've been watching you struggle, probably feeling helpless. Giving them specific ways to actually contribute rather than accidentally making things worse often makes things easier for everyone involved.

Teaching Your Family About OCD

You don't need to turn your support person into an OCD expert, but they do need to understand the basics. Here's the bare minimum they need to know:

OCD is like a faulty alarm clock. Your brain thinks there's danger when there isn't. The "alarm" blares, and you do compulsions to turn it off. But every time you turn off the alarm with compulsions, you're teaching your brain that there really *was* danger. So the alarm gets more sensitive.

Reassurance is like hitting the snooze button. It feels helpful in the moment, but it makes the problem worse long-term. When others reassure you, they're accidentally teaching your brain that uncertainty *is* dangerous and needs to be fixed.

Your job in treatment is to let the alarm go off without hitting snooze. Your family's job is to help you not hit snooze, even when you're begging them to.

That's it. You don't need to explain the neuroscience of habituation or the history of exposure therapy. Just: broken alarm, don't hit snooze, help me not hit snooze too.

If they're *interested* in learning more, you can always give them a copy of this book. (I'm imagining myself giving you a quick wink and a smile as I write this.)

How to Actually Ask for Help

Okay, so how do you actually have this conversation? Here's a script that works:

> *Hey [person], I need to talk to you about something. I'm working on my OCD, and part of my treatment involves changing how we interact when I'm anxious about [specific thing].*
>
> *Right now, when I ask you [specific reassurance question], you usually say [their typical response]. I know you're trying to help, and I really appreciate that you care about me. But reassurance actually makes my OCD stronger, even though it feels good in the moment.*
>
> *From now on, when I ask [specific question], I need you to say something like "I'm not going to answer that" or "That sounds like an OCD question" or even just "Maybe,*

maybe not." I know this is going to be hard for both of us, and I might get upset when you don't reassure me. But that's my OCD being mad, not me being mad at you.

Can you help me with this?

Notice what this script does:

- It's specific about what needs to change.
- It acknowledges that they mean well.
- It explains why reassurance is harmful.
- It gives them alternative responses.
- It warns them you might react badly initially.
- It asks for their help rather than demanding it.

When Your Support Person Actually Follows Through (Plot Twist!)

Okay, I know I'm making this sound like it's all sunshine and rainbows, but let me tell you what actually happens in real life.

You have this beautiful conversation with your support person about not giving you reassurance. They nod, they get it, they're totally on board. Then the next day, you ask them if they think you're contaminated, and they actually say, "Maybe, maybe not."

And you *completely* lose your mind.

Maybe you don't scream or throw things (though some

people do), but internally? You're having a full-blown panic attack. Your brain is screaming, "THEY'RE SUPPOSED TO CARE ABOUT ME! WHY WON'T THEY JUST TELL ME I'M OKAY?"

Your support person sees this. They watch you spiral, and their heart breaks a little. They're thinking, "Oh no, I'm making someone I care about suffer. This is awful. You know what? Forget the treatment plan. I'm just going to tell them they're fine so they know that I love them."

And we're back to square one.

Here's the thing: That freakout moment you're having? It doesn't just happen once. It becomes a pattern. You ask, they try to be strong and say maybe, you lose it, they cave and give reassurance, you feel better temporarily, and then the cycle starts all over again.

Eventually, your support person gets exhausted. They feel like they're constantly walking on eggshells, never knowing whether to help you or stick to the plan. They start feeling overwhelmed and confused about what the right thing to do is.

So here's your job. When they follow through with saying "Maybe, maybe not," don't punish them for it.

I know, I know. You're going to feel terrible when they don't reassure you. You might feel angry, abandoned, or panicked. That's normal. But instead of melting down (or if you do melt down, at least don't blame them for it), try to see this as an opportunity.

This is your chance to practice sitting with uncertainty while being grateful that someone loves you enough to watch you struggle for your own good. This is your exposure moment, handed to you on a silver platter.

You can sit there with all that anxiety and distress. Be mad, be scared, be whatever you need to be. But remember that your support person is doing the hard thing because they care about you. They're choosing your long-term recovery over your short-term comfort, which is actually incredibly loving, even when it doesn't feel that way.

And honestly, it's tough for them too. So maybe cut them some slack when they're brave enough to not give you the reassurance you're desperately wanting.

Setting Boundaries (a.k.a. Teaching People to Stop "Helping")

This is where things get tricky. Your family has probably developed habits around your OCD that they think are helpful. They might:

- Do tasks you avoid (like handling mail if you have contamination fears)
- Participate in your checking rituals ("Did you see me lock the door?")
- Provide reassurance, even without you asking ("That was a pothole, not a person.")
- Make accommodations to avoid triggering your OCD (preparing visitors beforehand to take shoes off when they arrive)

- Give you "updates" about things you worry about, even when you don't ask (texting "The kids are doing great" throughout the day)

All this comes from love. But it's also keeping your OCD alive.

You need to set boundaries around these behaviors. This doesn't mean being rude or ungrateful. It means being clear about what helps and what doesn't.

Some examples:

Instead of: "You never support me!"

Try: "I know you're trying to help, but when you check the locks for me, it actually makes my OCD worse. I need to practice not checking them myself."

Instead of: "Stop babying me!"

Try: "I appreciate that you've been handling the mail because of my contamination fears, but I need to start doing that myself as part of my treatment."

Instead of: "You're making my OCD worse!"

Try: "When I ask if you think I'm a bad person, can you remind me that's an OCD question instead of answering it?"

The key is being specific, acknowledging their good intentions, and explaining what you need instead.

The Daily Check-In System

One of the most practical things you can do is set up a daily check-in system with your support person. This isn't therapy. It's more like having a workout buddy for your brain.

Here's how it works:

1. **Pick a time.** Same time every day. Maybe seven p.m. after dinner, or right before bed. Something you can stick to.

2. **Keep it short.** We're talking one to two minutes max. This isn't a therapy session.

3. **Use the thumbs-up/thumbs-down system.**

    - Thumbs-up: What did you do well today with your OCD?
    - Thumbs-down: What could you improve tomorrow?

That's it. Super simple.

Example check-in:
You: "Thumbs-up: I touched three doorknobs today without washing my hands after."

Support person: "Nice work!"

You: "Thumbs-down: I asked you twice if I'm a good mom, even though we agreed I wouldn't do that."

Support person: "What are you going to do differently tomorrow?"

You: "When I have the urge to ask, I'll say, 'Maybe I'm a good mom, maybe I'm not' instead."

Support person: "Sounds like a plan."

Done. One minute. No analysis, no deep dives into feelings, no problem-solving together. Just accountability and forward focus. The beauty of this system is that it keeps your recovery front and center without making it the only thing you talk about.

What If You Keep Bringing Up the Same Struggles?

If you find yourself saying the same thumbs-down thing multiple days in a row, that's a red flag. You're probably not creating a real plan for change.

Support person: "This is the fourth day you've said you're struggling with asking for reassurance. What's going to be different tomorrow?"

You: "Um . . . I'll try harder?"

Nope. That's not a plan. That's a hope.

A real plan sounds like: "Tomorrow when I feel the urge to ask for reassurance, I'm going to immediately go do an exposure instead. If I'm in the kitchen and want to ask if I'm contaminated, I'll touch five more things without washing my hands."

If you can't come up with a specific plan for changing the behavior you keep struggling with, you're probably not ready to change it yet. And that's okay—just be honest about it.

Social Media: The Double-Edged Sword

Let's talk about the internet, because I know you're on there looking up your OCD symptoms. (I see you.)

Social media can be incredibly helpful for OCD recovery. It can also turn into the world's largest reassurance-seeking festival. The difference comes down to *why* you're posting or searching.

The Good Ways to Use Social Media for OCD

Sharing exposure wins: "Did my first public bathroom exposure today without excessive handwashing!" This celebrates progress and might inspire others.

Finding an exposure buddy: Someone who will check in with you about your daily exposures, cheer you on, and call you out when you're making excuses.

Learning about treatment: Reading research on ERP effectiveness, understanding different therapy approaches, finding qualified OCD specialists in your area.

Connecting with others who get it: Sometimes you need to talk to someone who understands that "Just stop worrying about it" isn't helpful advice.

The Problematic Ways to Use Social Media for OCD:

Asking for reassurance: "Does anyone else have thoughts about harming their kids?" "Is this contaminated?" "Do you think I'm a bad person?" These posts are seeking certainty and reassurance from strangers.

Sharing your OCD story for reassurance: Sometimes people share detailed accounts of their intrusive thoughts or feared scenarios, hoping others will tell them they're normal or okay.

Research spirals: Going down rabbit holes of what-if scenarios, symptom checking, or looking for the perfect explanation for your thoughts.

Comparison seeking: "My OCD is about contamination, but this person's is about harm thoughts, so maybe mine is worse/better/different."

The WTF Test

Before you post, comment, or search for something OCD-related online, ask yourself: "WTF?"

No . . . not that one. I mean, *What's the Function*?

What is the actual purpose of what you're about to do? What are you hoping to get out of it?

If the function is:

- To reduce anxiety
- To gain certainty
- To get reassurance

. . . then it's probably a compulsion, and you should step away from the keyboard.

If the function is:

- To share genuine progress
- To help someone else
- To find practical resources
- To connect with people who understand

. . . then it's probably helpful.

Finding Your Support Group or OCD Buddy

One of the best things you can do for your recovery is find other people who are also working on their OCD. This could be:

- **An in-person support group:** Check iocdf.org for groups near you. These usually meet monthly and focus on sharing progress and challenges.
- **An online support group:** Tons of forums and Facebook groups exist. But make sure they focus on treatment and recovery, not just venting about symptoms.
- **An OCD buddy:** This is like a workout partner for exposures. You check in with each other daily, share what exposures you're doing, and hold each other accountable.

The key is finding people who are actively working on recovery, not just talking about how hard OCD is. You want to surround yourself with people who are moving forward, not people who are stuck.

What to Look for in an OCD Buddy

- They're actively doing ERP or other evidence-based treatment.
- They understand that reassurance isn't helpful.

- They can celebrate your wins without making it about them.
- They can listen to your struggles without trying to fix them.
- They'll call you out (gently) when you're making excuses.

What Your OCD Buddy Should Not *Do*

- Give you reassurance about your specific fears
- Tell you your thoughts aren't real or don't matter
- Share their own detailed OCD stories in response to yours
- Try to convince you that you don't really have OCD
- Make it a competition about who has worse OCD

Setting Up Your Daily Buddy Check-In

If you find an OCD buddy, you can use the same thumbs-up/thumbs-down system we talked about earlier:

- **Text format:** 👍 "Held a knife while cooking dinner for 10 minutes." 👎 "Asked my husband for reassurance twice." "Tomorrow I'll bite my tongue when I want to ask and do an extra exposure instead."
- **Voice message format:** "Quick check-in: Thumbs-up, I did three contamination exposures today.

> Thumbs-down, I avoided the kitchen when my kids were hungry. Tomorrow I'm cooking breakfast no matter what thoughts show up."

Keep it brief, specific, and forward-focused.

When Family Members Get Tired of Helping

Supporting someone through OCD recovery can be exhausting. Your family might get tired of the role you are asking them to play. This is normal. They're human, and they love you, which makes watching you suffer difficult.

When family members start to burn out, it's time for an honest conversation:

"I know this has been hard on you too. I really appreciate you helping me with my recovery. Is there anything I can do to make this easier for you? Do you need a break from being my support person for a few days?"

Sometimes they just need acknowledgment that this is difficult for them too. Sometimes they need clearer boundaries about when they're "on duty" as your support person versus when they're just your family member. And sometimes, you need to find additional support so one person isn't carrying the whole load.

The Bottom Line

Getting your family involved in your OCD treatment isn't easy, but it's incredibly powerful when done right.

Your family wants to help. They've probably been trying to help in ways that accidentally make things worse. When you give them clear, specific ways to support your recovery, most people are relieved to finally know what to do.

And when you find that OCD buddy or support group? You'll discover you're not alone in this weird, challenging, totally doable journey toward freedom.

The people in your corner don't need to understand every detail of your OCD. They just need to understand that recovery is possible, that you're working hard, and that their job is to cheer you on while refusing to participate in OCD's games.

Chapter 15

What Can I Do Other Than Exposures?

We've now spent eleven chapters talking about ERP. I know some of you are probably thinking, "Okay, I get it. Exposures are important. Response prevention is crucial. But surely there's got to be something else I can do, right? Some other angle I can work? Maybe something a little . . . easier?"

I hear this question all the time. Here's what I need you to understand before we go any further: **ERP is nonnegotiable.** It's the gold standard for OCD treatment, and there's no getting around it. No amount of meditation, journaling, or positive thinking is going to rewire your brain the way exposures do.

But—and this is important—ERP doesn't have to be the *only* thing you do. Think of it like building a house. ERP is your foundation. Without it, everything else will crumble. But once you've got that solid foundation, you can add some helpful features that make the house more comfortable to live in.

So let's talk about what those "helpful features" might look like. Just remember, these are additions to ERP, not replacements for it.

The Truth About "Alternative" Treatments

I've seen too many people spend years bouncing from treatment to treatment, trying everything except the one thing that actually works. They'll try hypnosis, EMDR, energy healing, special diets, supplements, and about seventeen different types of meditation. Meanwhile, their OCD is sitting back, eating popcorn, watching them run around in circles.

Your brain is looking for an escape route from exposures. That's normal—exposures are hard! But there is no shortcut to freedom from OCD. The path goes straight through your fears, not around them.

That said, there are some approaches that can genuinely support your ERP work and make the whole journey a bit more manageable. Let's talk about those.

ACT: Learning to Surf the Waves

Acceptance and commitment therapy (ACT) is like ERP's laid-back cousin. While ERP teaches you to face your fears head-on, ACT teaches you to change your relationship with uncomfortable thoughts and feelings.

Think of it this way: If ERP is teaching you to dive into the ocean waves, ACT is teaching you how to surf them.

What ACT Is Really About

ACT operates on a simple but powerful idea. The problem isn't that you have difficult thoughts and feelings, it's that you're at war with them. Instead of fighting these internal experiences, ACT teaches you to make room for them while still living according to your values.

The core principle is psychological flexibility. This is your ability to stay present and engaged with your life even when your mind is throwing a tantrum. It's not about eliminating anxiety or intrusive thoughts (which is impossible anyway). It's about learning to carry them with you while still doing what matters.

How ACT Specifically Helps with OCD

Values clarification: Remember in chapter 6 when we talked about finding your why? ACT takes this even deeper. It helps you clarify what you actually care about, not what OCD tells you to care about.

ACT helps you distinguish between values (what you care about) and goals (what you want to achieve). Values are like directions—you can always move toward them. Goals are like destinations—you either reach them or you don't.

For example, "being a loving parent" is a value. "Never having a scary thought about my kids" is a goal that OCD has convinced you is necessary for being a loving parent. But they're completely different things.

When you're in the middle of a tough exposure, connecting

with your values can give you the strength to keep going. Instead of "I have to do this exposure to get rid of my thoughts," it becomes "I'm doing this exposure because I value being present and engaged with my family."

Cognitive defusion: This is a fancy way of saying "learning to see thoughts as just thoughts." If you've gotten this far in the book, some of these ACT-ified statements will sound awfully familiar to the work we've already covered:

- **Change the voice.** Say your obsessive thought in different voices, like Mickey Mouse, Darth Vader, or a robot. This breaks the thought's power by making it silly.

- **Sing it.** Take your scariest thought and sing it to the tune of "Happy Birthday" or any song you know. Hard to take it seriously when it's a jingle.

- **Add "I'm having the thought that . . ."** Instead of "I'm contaminated," say "I'm having the thought that I'm contaminated."

- **Thank your mind.** When an intrusive thought appears, say, "Hey, thanks for that thought man," like you're politely acknowledging a suggestion you're not going to take.

Mindful awareness: ACT helps you notice what's happening in your mind and body without immediately trying to fix it. This awareness can be incredibly helpful during exposures; you can observe your anxiety rising without automatically jumping into compulsions.

Here's how you might put this into practice:

- **Body scan check-ins:** When anxiety hits, quickly scan your body from head to toe. Notice: "My shoulders are tight, my stomach is churning, my hands are clenched." You're not trying to fix it, just observing. (Did you just rap this in your head like I did?)
- **The weather report:** Describe your internal experience like a weather forecast: "There's a storm of anxiety moving through, with scattered thoughts of contamination and a high pressure system of urgency."
- **Name it to tame it:** Simply label what's happening: "Obsessing," "Anxiety rising," "Urge to check." This creates distance.

Acceptance: This doesn't mean you like having OCD or that you're giving up. It means you stop fighting reality. Fighting your thoughts and feelings is like being in quicksand: The more you struggle, the deeper you sink.

Here are concrete ways to practice acceptance:

- **Stop saying, "I shouldn't feel this way."** Instead try: "This is what I'm feeling right now, and that's okay."
- **Use the phrase "This is hard *and* I can handle it."** You're not pretending it's easy, but you're also not catastrophizing.

- **Practice the "Yes, and . . ." technique.** "Yes, I'm having scary thoughts, and I can still make dinner." "Yes, I feel contaminated, and I can still hug my kids."

The Values vs. OCD Goals Exercise

Here's a practical ACT exercise to clarify your true values versus what OCD is telling you to value:

[Scan QR code.] →

Step 1: Identify what OCD says you "must" do or achieve. Examples:

- "To be a good person, I must never have impure thoughts."
- "To be safe, I must be 100 percent certain I'm not contaminated."
- "To be a good partner, I must never feel uncertainty about my relationship."

Step 2: Ask yourself, what's the underlying value? What do you actually care about beneath OCD's demands?

- "Never have impure thoughts" → Underlying value: "Being a person of integrity"
- "Complete certainty about contamination" → Underlying value: "Protecting my family's health"
- "No relationship uncertainty" → Underlying value: "Having authentic, loving connections"

Step 3: Find value-based actions you can take right now, even with OCD present.

- Instead of trying to eliminate impure thoughts, you could volunteer for a cause you care about.
- Instead of seeking contamination certainty, you could cook a meal for your family.
- Instead of analyzing your relationship, you could plan a fun activity with your partner.

Step 4: During exposures, connect with the value.

- "I'm allowing these unwanted thoughts because I value authenticity over the illusion of mental purity."
- "I'm doing this contamination exposure not to feel better, but because I value being present with my family without fear controlling me."

This exercise helps you see that you can live your values even while having OCD symptoms.

I mean, this has really always been the goal. Whether you're having very few symptoms or a massive amount, you can still do the things that bring you joy.

How ACT Works with ERP

ACT doesn't replace exposures—it gives you better tools for doing them. When you're in the middle of an exposure and anxiety is spiking, ACT skills help you stay present instead of getting lost in the panic. You learn to ride the wave of anxiety instead of getting tumbled by it.

Mindfulness: The Art of Paying Attention

Mindfulness has become such a buzzword that it's practically meaningless now. Everyone from your yoga instructor to your dentist is talking about it. But when used correctly alongside ERP, mindfulness can be genuinely helpful.

What Mindfulness Actually Is (and Isn't)

Mindfulness isn't about clearing your mind or achieving some Zen state. It's not about feeling peaceful or relaxed (though those things might happen). It's simply about paying attention to what's happening right now, without trying to change it.

Think of mindfulness as if you're a scientist studying your own experience. You're observing what's happening in your mind and body with curiosity rather than judgment.

The Mindfulness Attitude

True mindfulness involves several key attitudes:

- **Nonjudgmental awareness:** Noticing what's happening without labeling it as "good" or "bad"
- **Beginner's mind:** Approaching each moment with fresh eyes, as if experiencing it for the first time

- **Acceptance:** Allowing things to be as they are right now
- **Non-striving:** Not trying to get anywhere or achieve any particular state
- **Letting go:** Not holding on to pleasant experiences or pushing away unpleasant ones

Where Mindfulness Specifically Helps with OCD

Catching compulsions before they happen: Many compulsions happen on autopilot. You're washing your hands before you even realize you decided to do it. Mindfulness gives you that split second of awareness when you can choose differently.

One simple way to build this skill: Set a few random alarms on your phone throughout the day. When they go off, just ask yourself, "What am I doing right now? Am I about to do a compulsion?" That tiny pause often reveals whether you're acting from choice or from OCD. We're simply trying to bring awareness to patterns in your day.

Sitting with discomfort: This is probably mindfulness's biggest gift to OCD recovery. You learn that uncomfortable feelings won't kill you, even though they feel like they might.

When anxiety hits, instead of immediately trying to make it go away, try this: Notice where you feel it in your body. Is your chest tight? Stomach churning? Just observe it for sixty seconds like you're a researcher studying a curious phenomenon. Often that's enough for the urgent need to "do something" to pass.

Breaking out of mental loops: OCD loves to get you stuck analyzing, reviewing, trying to figure things out. Mindfulness helps you step out of these loops by anchoring you in the present moment.

When you catch yourself in a mental spiral, try naming it: "Worrying" or "Analyzing" or even just "Loop, loop, loop." Don't say whether it's good or bad. Then deliberately focus on something physical—your feet on the ground, sounds around you, your breath. You're not fighting the thoughts; you're just choosing where to put your attention.

Mindfulness Tool: The STOP Technique

When you notice OCD ramping up, try this simple mindfulness practice:

S: Stop what you're doing. Literally pause. I don't care if you're mid-sentence in a conversation or halfway through washing your hands. Just freeze for a second.

T: Take a breath. One conscious, intentional breath. Nothing complicated, just one normal breath that you focus on. Feel the air coming in, feel it going out. This gives your nervous system a tiny reset.

O: Observe what's happening right now without trying to fix anything. Ask yourself:

- What thoughts are bouncing around in my head right now?
- What emotions am I feeling? (Anxiety? Disgust? Panic?)

- What's happening in my body? (Tight chest? Clenched jaw? Sweaty palms?)
- What urges am I having? (To wash? To check? To ask for reassurance?)

You're not judging any of this as good or bad. You're just collecting information.

P: Proceed with awareness. Here's where you get to choose. Now that you know what's happening, what do you want to do next? You can still choose to do a compulsion if you want, but now it's a conscious choice rather than an automatic reaction.

This isn't about making anxiety go away. It's about inserting a moment of choice between the trigger and your response. Sometimes that tiny pause is all you need to choose differently.

The more you practice STOP, the bigger that pause becomes. Eventually, you might find yourself naturally pausing before compulsions without even thinking about it.

DBT Skills: Your Emotional Tool Kit

Dialectical behavior therapy (DBT) was originally developed for people with intense emotional experiences, but some of its skills are incredibly useful for OCD recovery.

DBT is like having a Swiss Army knife for emotional situations. It gives you practical tools for managing intense feelings without making things worse.

Understanding DBT's Approach

DBT is built on the idea that you can't think your way out of an emotional crisis—you need concrete skills. It's incredibly practical and focuses on what works, not what sounds good in theory.

The "dialectical" part means holding two seemingly opposite truths at the same time. For example: "I hate feeling this anxious *and* I can handle it." Or "This exposure is terrifying *and* it's exactly what I need to do."

Three Key DBT Modules and How They Help with OCD

Distress tolerance: This is about surviving crisis moments without doing things that make the situation worse (like compulsions). When you're at that **8/10** anxiety level and desperate to do a compulsion, you need something to bridge the gap until the intensity passes.

These are things like doing jumping jacks, splashing cold water on your face, or running around your house one time.

Now, I need to address something controversial here. Some OCD specialists worry that distress tolerance techniques might become mini-compulsions—ways to avoid feeling anxiety rather than sitting with it. And they're not wrong to be concerned.

Here's the key difference: If you're using these techniques to eliminate anxiety or because you believe something bad will happen if you don't, then yes, they've become compulsions. But if you're using them to stay functional enough to resist your actual compulsions, that's different.

The goal isn't comfort. The goal is function. These techniques should help you tolerate uncertainty, not eliminate it.

Emotion regulation: This helps you understand what sets off your emotions and how to ride them out. For example, you might notice that your contamination fears spike when you're tired, or your relationship doubts get worse when you're stressed at work.

Once you spot these patterns, you can prepare for them. If you know Sunday evenings trigger your OCD, you might plan some self-care or schedule exposures for that time.

Interpersonal effectiveness: If your OCD involves relationships, this teaches you how to communicate without making things worse. Instead of asking, "Do you think I'm a bad person?" for the tenth time today, you learn to say something like "I'm having a rough OCD day and might need some extra patience."

DBT Tool: The TIPP Technique for Emotional Crisis

When anxiety is overwhelming and you're tempted to do compulsions, try TIPP:

T: Temperature: Change your body temperature quickly to shift your emotional state. Splash cold water on your face, hold ice cubes, take a hot shower, or step outside if it's cold. This works because extreme temperatures activate your parasympathetic nervous system, which naturally calms your body.

I: Intense exercise: Do jumping jacks, run up and down stairs, do push-ups, or sprint around the block. Physical intensity burns off stress chemicals and gives your emotions somewhere to go.

P: Paced breathing: Breathe out longer than you breathe in. Try four counts in, six counts out. This activates your body's relaxation response.

P: Progressive muscle relaxation: Tense and release muscle groups, starting with your toes and working up to your head.

Use TIPP when you're at an **8/10** or higher distress level and on the verge of doing compulsions. These techniques aren't meant to eliminate anxiety, they're meant to bring your distress down just enough so you can think clearly and make better choices. You're buying yourself time to let the urge to do compulsions pass.

What I don't want someone to do is say, "Oh no, I'm feeling anxious, I better go take a cold shower." It's not something you *have* to do. It's something you're *choosing* to do, and if you do . . . can you guess what follows? An exposure. These skills prepare you to be in a better space for ERP.

Behavioral Activation: My Favorite

Behavioral activation sounds complex, but in truth it's pretty simple: Start doing stuff that matters to you, even when you don't feel like it.

This approach comes from depression research, but it's incredibly relevant for OCD because both conditions can make you withdraw from life.

The Problem OCD Creates

OCD loves to shrink your world. It convinces you to avoid more and more activities, people, and experiences. You might stop cooking because of contamination fears, avoid social events because of reassurance-seeking urges, or quit hobbies because they trigger obsessions.

Pretty soon, your life revolves entirely around managing OCD instead of actually living. Your world gets smaller and smaller until you're just surviving, not thriving.

The Behavioral Activation Approach

Instead of waiting until you "feel better" to start living your life, you start living your life in order to feel better. It's the opposite of what most people think recovery looks like.

The idea is that behavior change leads to mood change, not the other way around. When you start doing meaningful activities again, your mood and motivation follow.

How This Specifically Helps with OCD

Reduces rumination time: When your life is full of meaningful activities, OCD has less space to operate. It's harder for obsessions to take over when you're actively engaged in things you care about.

Natural exposure opportunities: Behavioral activation often naturally creates exposure situations. If you used to love cooking but avoid it because of contamination fears, returning to cooking becomes both behavioral activation *and* exposure practice.

Builds mastery and confidence: Accomplishing meaningful tasks—even small ones—builds your confidence and reminds you that you're capable of more than just managing OCD.

Reconnects you with your values: When you start doing things you care about again, you remember what you're fighting for.

How to Use Behavioral Activation

You can think of behavioral activation as a way to do things you haven't done in a while or to try new things. It can be taking something you already do and adding something new to it.

You may take out a calendar and set up activities that you're going to do every day.

Here are some examples:

- Text an old friend.
- Join a club or group.
- Take a walk around the block.
- Go to the gym.
- Dance to music in your living room.
- Write in a journal.
- Try a craft project.
- Learn something new online.
- Fix something that's been broken.
- Try a new recipe.
- Volunteer for a cause you care about.

- Help a neighbor.
- Attend a religious service.

[Scan QR code.] →

Pick activities that used to bring you joy, even if they don't sound appealing right now. Action creates motivation, not the other way around.

Here's where many get it wrong. They do the activity as just something to check off their list. Instead, we want to make it very meaningful. You're not just going somewhere to volunteer, you're creating goals for yourself. "When I'm there, I'm going to say hi to two people and compliment another."

You may need to get creative for how to make what you're doing meaningful. If you read every day, try switching up locations, texting a friend about what you've read, or drawing a character from the book afterward. We're not looking for skill here, just that you're doing something new or different.

Do it regardless of how you feel. This is crucial. Don't wait until you feel motivated or until your anxiety is low. Do it *especially* when you don't feel like it.

Notice what happens. How do you feel during and after? What did you learn? What was different than you expected?

If you can get back to things you stopped doing, that's even better.

Again, action creates motivation, not the other way around.

The Doctor Just Wants to Throw Meds at Me

Let's talk about the elephant in the room: medication.

I'm not a medical doctor, and I can't prescribe medication. But I can share some information from research and my observations working with clients who take medication for OCD.

What the Research Actually Shows

Certain medications can be effective for reducing OCD symptoms. The most common are SSRIs (selective serotonin reuptake inhibitors), like Prozac, Zoloft, Paxil, Luvox, and others.

Studies show that about seven out of ten people who try these medications see significant symptom reduction—somewhere between 40 and 60 percent improvement. That's pretty good odds, but it's not a magic cure.

Here's the crucial part even many doctors don't know: The medications that help with OCD typically need to be taken at much higher doses than what's used for depression. We're talking doses that might make a depression specialist nervous, but they're completely appropriate for OCD.

For example, Prozac for depression might be twenty milligrams daily. For OCD, the effective dose is often forty to eighty milligrams daily. Many people don't get relief because they're only taking depression doses. Then they stop taking them and say, "Medication never worked for me," not knowing they weren't even close to the therapeutic dose.

The Medication Timeline

Unlike some medications that work quickly, OCD medications typically take eight to twelve weeks to show their full effect. Some people see improvement earlier, but you really need to give it time.

This is frustrating when you're suffering, but it's important to know so you don't give up too early.

How Medication Might Help with ERP

ERP is like learning to play a video game on the hardest setting. It's brutal at first, but it forces you to develop real skills. Medication is like turning down the difficulty level from expert to intermediate. If you use medication to make ERP more manageable, you're still building those core skills, just with less-overwhelming anxiety. And once you've mastered the game mechanics, you can handle whatever level you're playing on.

Medication may also help with the depression and hopelessness that often accompany OCD, giving you more energy to tackle treatment.

I think about OCD as handcuffing you, making you feel trapped. Taking medication may unlock one of the cuffs, still leaving you bound, but ERP unlocks the other, giving you total freedom and a better shot at doing treatment.

What Medication Can't Do

Medication alone typically isn't enough for lasting recovery. It might reduce your symptoms, but it won't teach your brain the new patterns that ERP creates. Most people who rely only on medication find that their symptoms return if they stop taking it.

Medication is like a crutch for a broken leg. It's incredibly helpful for healing, but you still need to do physical therapy to get your strength back.

Side Effects and Considerations

Like all medications, OCD medications can have side effects. Common ones include nausea, headaches, sexual side effects, and weight changes. Most of these are temporary and improve as your body adjusts.

So . . . Nate, should I take a medication?

I know you want my opinion, and I'll give it to you straight.

YOU MIGHT NEED MEDICATION IF:

- Your OCD symptoms are severe and significantly interfere with daily functioning.
- You've tried ERP but can't engage with it effectively due to overwhelming anxiety.
- You have co-occurring depression that's making OCD treatment difficult.
- Your symptoms take up more than a few hours per day.
- You're at risk for self-injury or suicide.
- Your quality of life is severely impacted despite trying other approaches.

MEDICATION MIGHT NOT BE RIGHT FOR YOU IF:

- Your OCD symptoms are mild to moderate and you can engage in ERP effectively.
- You're making good progress with ERP alone.
- You have concerns about side effects that outweigh potential benefits.
- You prefer to try psychological approaches first.
- You have medical conditions that make OCD medications risky.
- You're able to function reasonably well in daily activities.
- Your support system is strong and you have access to good ERP treatment.

Here's the dealio. There is no "right" choice. You've got to do what works for you. If someone comes in my office and is not on medication, I don't push for them to get it. We do ERP first and see how it goes.

I've seen people start medications and it changed their whole demeanor. They became happy and confident, and the fears weren't as strong as they'd been.

I've also seen some start and the side effects were too overwhelming.

Here's a statement I often hear from patients: "I'm kicking myself for not starting this sooner. It's life-changing."

At the end of the day, the phrase that continues to come

to my mind about medications is "Maybe they will help and maybe they won't." (You see what I did there?)

If you're considering medication, work with a psychiatrist who understands OCD and is familiar with the higher doses typically needed.

What About Everything Else?

"But what about [insert treatment here]?" you might be asking. "I heard EMDR works for trauma, and my OCD started after a traumatic event."

"What about hypnosis? My cousin's friend's neighbor tried it and said it cured their OCD."

"What about special diets? I read that sugar feeds anxiety."

Here's my take on all the other approaches people try:

Ketamine: This one actually has some real research behind it. A small study found that half the people who got ketamine had significant improvement in their OCD symptoms within a week, while none of the people who got the placebo improved.

What's cool about ketamine is how fast it works. Some people feel relief within ten minutes of receiving it. That's way different from regular medications, which can take months to kick in. (But my therapist tingles are kicking in here, flagging a possible compulsion when I hear how *fast* it works.)

The research is still pretty limited. Most studies have been tiny (like, fifteen people), and we need to look at much bigger populations to really know if it works. Plus, ketamine can be addictive and has some gnarly side effects.

This is only for people whose OCD hasn't responded to the usual treatments. It's not something you'd try first.

Psychedelics/microdosing: This is the hot new thing in OCD research, but we're still in the very early stages. Places like Yale and Imperial College London are conducting studies with psilocybin (magic mushrooms) for OCD.

One tiny study in 2006 (nine people) found that psilocybin helped reduce OCD symptoms in some people. And there are surveys in which people say psychedelics helped their OCD. Larger randomized controlled trials are now underway, including a thirty-person study at Yale. Early results continue to show promise.

But—and this is a big but—the research is super limited. These are carefully controlled medical studies, not people doing psychedelics at home.

To me, it feels like we're reaching for anything at this point to reduce OCD symptoms, and this wouldn't be my go-to intervention.

TMS (transcranial magnetic stimulation): This one has some promising evidence to support it, and the FDA approved TMS for OCD in 2018.

Basically, TMS uses magnetic pulses to stimulate specific parts of your brain. It can help some people whose OCD hasn't responded to the usual treatments. In a study of one hundred people with *treatment-resistant* OCD, 38 percent who got real TMS had significant improvement (their symptoms dropped by at least 30 percent) compared with only 11 percent who got fake TMS (placebo).

But here's the thing: It's expensive, you need daily sessions for weeks, and it's definitely not a first choice. You'd only consider this if ERP and medication haven't worked for you.

If you're thinking about TMS, make sure you've really given ERP a solid try first.

EMDR: Eye movement desensitization and reprocessing uses eye movements to help process trauma. But OCD isn't caused by unprocessed traumatic memories—it's caused by a brain that's stuck in a false alarm pattern. While some research suggests that EMDR may help with OCD symptoms, ERP remains the gold-standard treatment with the strongest research support.

Even if trauma triggered your OCD, treating the trauma alone may not fully resolve OCD symptoms. They're separate issues that may need separate approaches.

Hypnosis: Some people find it relaxing, but relaxation isn't the same as recovery. You can't hypnotize your way out of OCD any more than you can hypnotize your way out of diabetes.

Hypnosis might help you feel calmer temporarily, but it won't change the underlying patterns that keep OCD alive.

Talk therapy/psychoanalysis: Traditional talk therapy, in which you explore your childhood and try to understand why you have OCD, typically doesn't help with these symptoms. Understanding why won't change your brain patterns.

It's like trying to cure a phobia of spiders by talking about your relationship with your mother. Interesting conversation, but the spider phobia will still be there.

I-CBT (inference-based CBT): This approach claims you can treat OCD by challenging the reasoning behind your obsessions instead of doing exposures. It sounds appealing because who wouldn't want to skip the scary stuff and just think their way out of OCD?

The idea is that obsessions aren't random intrusive thoughts. They're based on faulty reasoning. So instead of doing exposures, you learn to question the logic behind your obsessive doubts and strengthen "reality-based reasoning."

Unlike some of these other approaches, I-CBT actually has *some* decent research behind it. A few randomized controlled trials found it works about as well as standard CBT. One study even found people tolerated it better than regular CBT (probably because there are no exposures).

But here's my concern: It feels like we are attempting to out-logic OCD, which is like trying to reason with a toddler having a meltdown.

That said, some people say they genuinely do better with I-CBT, especially those who struggle to recognize their OCD thoughts as unreasonable or who truly believe their fears might be realistic. If you've tried ERP multiple times with proper guidance and feel it's not working, I-CBT might be worth considering. Just don't use it as an excuse to avoid the hard work indefinitely.

Special diets/supplements: I've seen people try gluten-free diets, sugar elimination, specific supplements, and various "detoxes." While overall health matters, there's no special diet that cures OCD. Some people report feeling slightly better when they eat well and exercise, but it's not a treatment for the disease.

Putting It All Together: Your Complete Recovery Plan

So what does a complete OCD recovery plan look like? Here's how all these pieces might fit together:

Monday morning: *You do your planned exposure (touching a public doorknob without washing your hands). When anxiety spikes, you use the ACT ("I'm having the thought") technique to create distance from your contamination fears. You remind yourself of your values (being present for your family) to stay motivated.*

Tuesday evening: *Anxiety is really high after a tough day. You use the DBT TIPP technique to bring your distress down from a* 9/10 *to a* 6/10, *making it easier to resist compulsions and bringing more motivation to follow it up with an exposure. You also make sure to engage in a meaningful activity (calling a friend) as part of your behavioral activation plan instead of isolating.*

Wednesday: *You notice your mind trying to analyze and "figure out" your obsessions. You use mindfulness to observe this mental loop without getting caught in it, then return your attention to what you're actually doing.*

See how everything works together? ERP is doing the heavy lifting—actually rewiring your brain's response to uncertainty. The other approaches are supporting that work by giving you better tools for navigating the process.

A Word of Caution

I need to be straight with you about something: Your OCD is going to try to turn these supporting approaches into compulsions.

It might convince you that you need to meditate for exactly twenty minutes every day or your anxiety will spike. It might turn mindfulness into a ritual in which you have to notice exactly five things around you before you can move on. It might make you believe that if you don't do your breathing exercises perfectly, something bad will happen.

Watch out for this. The moment any tool starts feeling mandatory or ritualized, step back and reassess. Are you using it to enhance your life, or are you using it to avoid anxiety?

The Bottom Line

The most important thing to remember is that ERP is the foundation of your recovery. Everything else is just a bonus.

Do not use this chapter as an excuse to avoid exposures. Your brain is incredibly good at finding reasons to delay the hard work. Don't let it trick you into thinking you need to master mindfulness before you can start doing exposures, or that you need the perfect medication before you can face your fears.

Start with ERP. Do it imperfectly. Do it scared. Do it even when you don't want to. Then, if these other approaches call to you, add them in as supporting players.

Chapter 16

Your Turn to Take Back Your Life

I've seen hundreds of people with OCD throughout my career. I've watched some people absolutely crush it and get their lives back. I've seen others struggle, make excuses, and stay stuck. The difference isn't how smart they are, how severe their OCD is, or how long they've had it.

The difference is action.

So let me tell you what works, what doesn't work, and what you need to hear right now if you want to kick OCD to the curb and get your life back.

Treatment Works. Period.

Whether you're new to OCD or you've been struggling for years, let me be crystal clear about something. There *is* treatment that works: Exposure and Response Prevention (ERP). We've covered it extensively in this book, but I want to drive this point home one more time.

Your brain is throwing out false signals and wants you to react to them. What we're going to do is take those false signals and say, "Cool, let me go face that thing you told me is really important. And I'm going to respond completely differently about it. Let me show you just how much I don't care."

ERP is hard work. Your brain is really good at saying, "Don't go do that. You tried it once and it was horrible. It's probably not the thing for you."

Why does your brain suggest these alternatives? Because they're easier. They don't require you to face your fears head-on. But easy isn't always best. I can almost guarantee that if you do exposures consistently and correctly, they're going to help you in some way.

People wait for the right moment. "Okay, I just finished Nate's book, but I can't start exposures until I see a therapist." Uhhhh, wrong. Have confidence in yourself. Fail at doing exposures and learn from the experiences. It's better than doing nothing at all.

Frequency Matters More Than You Think

Here's where most people mess up: They do exposures, but they don't do them enough.

Exposures must be done daily. Not for a few minutes, but much longer, possibly even hours. How much time are you spending obsessing about something or doing compulsions? Count up all those minutes. I bet we could replace them with exposures.

I know you're busy. You've got work, school, kids to take care of, whatever, whatever, whatever. But it will not get better unless you do it often.

I love calendars. I want you to write out specific exposures you're going to do: 7:00 A.M., 10:00 A.M., 11:00 A.M., 12:00 P.M., 1:00 P.M. "I'm going to look at this picture and sit there for twenty minutes if I have to, until that anxiety goes down, then move on with my life. I'm going to do it again. And again. And again."

The people who just buckle down and say, "I'm doing this thing, I don't care, I'm risking it all," are the ones who get better.

Many people hear "Do hours of exposures a day" and instantly think, "I can't," and never try. Remember, this isn't an all-or-nothing thing. If you're doing a few minutes of exposures a day, it doesn't mean that you can't get better. *Do something!*

You Need Support (Whether You Want It or Not)

Find a support person. I don't care if it's your mom, dad, friend, spouse, or whoever. You've got to tell them what you're doing.

"If I'm sitting on the couch playing video games and you hear my timer going off and I'm not standing up to go do my exposure, kick me." (Hopefully they won't actually kick you and will just remind you what you committed to.)

People don't want support, but they need it. It's like going to the gym: If you have somebody expecting you to show up, you're going to do better than if you're just lying in bed at six a.m. thinking, "Nah, I'll go back to sleep."

Find a support person. I know it feels annoying, but they can help. They probably would love to help. They want you to get better.

There's Never a Perfect Time to Start

There is not a great time to do treatment. There's always an excuse: "I've got a job," "I've got kids," "I've got [fill in the blank]."

Don't wait for the best time to do it. You're not going to feel ready. You just have to do it.

Break *All* Your Compulsions

Be aware of your compulsions, and stop holding on to those one or two that you're just unwilling to break. You need to break them all.

People do this all the time: "I'm doing so much better! I'll just keep doing what I'm doing even if I'm holding on to a few compulsions."

No. Let's see if we can break all of them. We don't have to do it all right now, but I need you to break all of them eventually.

Be honest with yourself about this. Write down all the compulsions you do: asking for reassurance, ruminating, problem-solving, going to forums every day to figure stuff out, checking, tapping, praying "just to be safe."

Let's break them. It's going to feel awful, but let's do it.

The Medication Truth

Always talk to your prescriber before taking anything, of course. But medication can be life-changing.

Everyone fights it at first, but I can't even tell you how many times I've heard someone say, "I started medication and I'm feeling way better. My obsessions went from all day to barely any."

Of course, there are outliers, like people who experience side effects or don't respond well. But you never know until you try it, especially when you're doing a lot of obsessions and compulsions all day long.

I'm not going to scream at you to take medication, because I want you to make your own decision. But in my brain, I'm thinking "Yes, yes, yes, go, go, go!" because I know it's going to help most people feel better.

Here's what's important: Have realistic expectations. A lot of people say, "I tried it and it never worked for me." But medication isn't an all-or-nothing thing. You've got to take the medication *and* do the treatment.

Find Professional Help If You Can

See a therapist if you can. I know that's not an option for everyone. Go to iocdf.org to find an excellent trained specialist.

If that's not possible, that's exactly why I wrote this book. But if you can work with someone who specializes in OCD, do it.

Maintenance Is Forever (and That's Okay)

After treatment, you've got to maintain the progress you've made. You don't just do ERP and be done forever. It's like going to the gym. I'm not going to get really strong and then say, "I'm done, never going back." Nah, it doesn't work that way.

Can you do something every day that reminds you that this used to be hard for you? Whether it's touching something, looking at an image, doing a certain behavior, or saying a certain word, it's something that says, "Nuh-uh, not anymore. This used to be a problem and I'm not letting it come back."

That's what maintenance is, and I want you doing it every day.

Live Your Life

Here's the cool part: Live life. Even if you don't feel like it, live it. Go do it. Because that's the whole point of OCD recovery.

Just go do the things you want to do. Stop avoiding. Stop waiting until you feel better. Do it now, even with OCD along for the ride if it wants to come along. (You're just not reacting to it.)

What Recovery Actually Looks Like

Recovery looks different for each person. I've had patients get to a point where OCD barely whispers in the background. Others still notice thoughts but can shrug them off like annoying ads on their phone.

Some people find that their anxiety drops dramatically. Others learn to function with anxiety present. Both are wins.

The goal isn't to never have another intrusive thought or feel anxious again. The goal is to not let these feelings control your life.

Recovery means different things:

- Maybe you still have the thoughts sometimes, but you can cook dinner anyway.
- Maybe you still feel anxious, but you don't spend an hour checking locks.
- Maybe you still notice triggers, but you don't rearrange your whole day to avoid them.
- Maybe you still have bad days, but you have way more good days.

That's real recovery. Not some fantasy version in which you never struggle again, but a real life in which struggles don't run the show.

Trust the Process

I know this is hard. I know there are days when you'll want to quit, when it feels like too much, when OCD convinces you that you're the exception to the rule.

You're not.

Trust the process. Take ownership of your journey. Stop looking for permission to start, stop waiting for the perfect moment, stop making excuses.

The tools in this book work. I've seen them work more times than I can count. But they work *only* if you use them.

Your Turn

I hope I didn't come off as too direct, but I want you to feel better. You have so much potential and joy to bring to others. Stop messing around with the slow stuff. Hit it fast, stay committed.

I know beyond a shadow of a doubt that people get better and live the life they want to live.

It's literally your turn now.

Sarah walks into my office for what we both know will be our last session. She's carrying a grocery bag and wearing a huge smile.

"I made dinner last night," she announces, setting the bag on the chair beside her. "Chicken stir-fry. With a really sharp knife. While my kids were helping me cook."

"How'd it go?" I ask, though her expression already tells me everything.

"The thoughts came," she says matter-of-factly. "Those scary ones about the knife. But I just said, 'Ohhhh . . . I'm so scared, maybe I'll snap,' and kept chopping vegetables. My daughter asked why I was smiling while cooking, and I told her it was because I was happy to be making dinner for people I love."

She pulls something out of the bag: a container of leftovers. "I brought you some. Because this represents everything I thought I'd never be able to do again."

I accept the container, genuinely touched. "This is incredible, Sarah."

"The coolest part?" she continues. "Yesterday, my brain tried to throw a new theme at me. Suddenly I was worried about whether I'd accidentally shoplifted at the grocery store. The old me would have panicked, driven back to check the security cameras, called the store manager to confess something I didn't even do."

"And the new you?"

"The new me rolled my eyes and said, 'Nice try, OCD. Maybe I did steal something, maybe I didn't. Guess we'll never know for sure.' Then I went home and made that stir-fry."

I grin. "Are you telling me that I may become an accessory to a crime by accepting your leftovers?"

I take the container anyway, holding it up like evidence. "Well . . . if I'm going down, at least I'll have stir-fry on the way."

As Sarah gathers her things to leave, she pauses at the door.

"You know what's funny? I used to think recovery meant never having another scary thought. Now I know it means having those thoughts and not caring about them anymore."

That's it right there. That's what recovery looks like.

Yes, we've talked about Sarah's specific themes throughout this book, contamination fears that evolved into harm thoughts. But the tools she learned to use? They work for you too, regardless of what your OCD looks like.

The "Maybe, maybe not" response she mastered works whether your brain is worried about germs, harm, relationships, morality, or anything else.

The exposure work she did? Same principle applies to every OCD theme.

The response prevention techniques? Universal.

Your OCD might wear a different mask than Sarah's, but underneath, it's the same disorder playing the same tricks. And that means the same tools that set her free can set you free too.

So here's my final challenge to you: Stop reading about recovery and start living it. Stop analyzing your thoughts and start facing your fears. Stop waiting for permission and start taking action.

Your life is waiting for you on the other side of those fears you've been avoiding.

Go get it.

Acknowledgments

Writing a book about OCD while maintaining a practice, running online courses, and creating YouTube content is . . . well, let's just say my OCD clients would recognize the irony of me trying to do everything perfectly. This book exists because of the incredible people who supported me and occasionally reminded me to take a break.

First and foremost, thank you to Gina, my wife and partner in all things. You've listened to me talk about intrusive thoughts and uncertainty tolerance for over a decade without once suggesting I find a different career. Your support and patience made this book possible. I love you.

To my three kids—thank you for understanding that even though I was home, I actually had work to do. Your patience means everything. Watching you grow up reminds me why helping families affected by OCD matters so much.

And to Gunner, who kept my feet warm during countless writing sessions.

To my editor, Nick—thank you for believing this message needed to reach beyond YouTube.

To the team at Penguin Random House—thank you for believing in this project and for your patience with my insistence on keeping things conversational. Special thanks for understanding that sometimes "maybe, maybe not" really is the best answer we can give.

To my colleagues and mentors in the OCD treatment community—your dedication to evidence-based care has shaped everything I do. To those who taught me that the gold standard isn't talk therapy or reassurance, but the hard work of exposure—thank you.

To the thousands of students in my Master Your OCD course and the millions who have watched my YouTube channel, OCD and Anxiety—your questions revealed gaps in my explanations, your struggles showed me where treatment needed clarity, and your successes reminded me why all of this matters.

To my clients over the past fifteen-plus years—watching you face your OCD with courage and reclaim your lives never gets old. You are the reason I know recovery is possible.

To the researchers who figured out that Exposure and Response Prevention works—this book stands on the foundation you built.

To my parents—thank you for supporting my decision to become a therapist.

To my friends who made fun of my video thumbnails and roasted my latest uploads—your support disguised as mockery is exactly the kind of friendship I need.

And finally, to everyone who is reading this and struggling with OCD—I see you. I know you're exhausted. I know you've wondered if recovery is even possible for you.

Your fight takes real bravery—the kind that doesn't get recognized, because it happens in your head. Recovery is possible. You deserve it. And you're not alone.

Appendix

Further Resources for Managing Your OCD

Find a Therapist

International OCD Foundation (IOCDF)

iocdf.org

The leading organization for OCD, offering a therapist directory to find specialized OCD treatment providers, support groups, educational materials, and an annual conference. IOCDF provides evidence-based information for individuals with OCD and their families.

NOCD

treatmyocd.com

Online therapy platform offering video sessions with licensed therapists specializing in Exposure and Response Prevention for OCD. Available in all fifty states and internationally.

Online Resources

Master Your OCD Online Course

ocd-anxiety.com

Comprehensive online course covering ERP treatment strategies for all OCD themes.

OCD and Anxiety YouTube Channel

youtube.com/ocdandanxiety

Educational videos on OCD themes, treatment strategies, and recovery.

Crisis Resources

If you're in crisis, please reach out to a mental health professional or crisis service in your area. In the United Kingdom, you can call 0800 587 0800 (National Suicide Prevention Helpline) or 116 123 (Samaritans).

Recommended Reading

For Adults with OCD

The Self-Compassion Workbook for OCD by Kimberley Quinlan, LMFT

Everyday Mindfulness for OCD by Jon Hershfield, MFT, and Shala Nicely, LPC

The OCD Answer Book by Patrick B. McGrath, PhD

The Compulsive Reassurance Seeking Workbook by Amanda Petrik-Gardner, LCPC (foreword by Nathan Peterson, LCSW)

The Mental Compulsions Workbook for OCD by Lauren K. M. Rosen, LMFT

Getting Over OCD by Jonathan S. Abramowitz, PhD

Overcoming Unwanted Intrusive Thoughts by Sally M. Winston, PsyD, and Martin N. Seif, PhD

Stop Obsessing! by Edna B. Foa, PhD, and Reid Wilson, PhD

Worrying Is Optional by Ben Eckstein, LCSW

For Parents and Families

Freeing Your Child from Obsessive-Compulsive Disorder by Tamar E. Chansky, PhD

Talking Back to OCD by John S. March, MD, and Christine M. Benton

When a Family Member Has OCD by Jon Hershfield, MFT

For Children

What to Do When You Have a Tricky, Sticky, Picky Brain by Marni L. Jacob, PhD

What to Do When Your Brain Gets Stuck by Dawn Huebner, PhD

Up and Down the Worry Hill by Aureen Pinto Wagner, PhD

Additional Resources

For a comprehensive list of books, treatment centers, and educational materials, visit the International OCD Foundation at iocdf.org.

About the Author

Nathan Peterson, LCSW, is a Texas-based clinician specializing in OCD. His YouTube channel, OCD and Anxiety, is the platform's most popular channel devoted to OCD content. This is his first book.